writing for

publication

The Academic's Support Kit

Building your Academic Career
Rebecca Boden, Debbie Epstein and Jane Kenway

Getting Started on Research
Rebecca Boden, Jane Kenway and Debbie Epstein

Writing for Publication
Debbie Epstein, Jane Kenway and Rebecca Boden

Teaching and Supervision
Debbie Epstein, Rebecca Boden and Jane Kenway

Winning and Managing Research Funding
Jane Kenway, Rebecca Boden and Debbie Epstein

Building Networks
Jane Kenway, Debbie Epstein and Rebecca Boden

writing for
publication

Debbie **Epstein**

Jane **Kenway**

Rebecca **Boden**

SAGE Publications
London • Thousand Oaks • New Delhi

First published 2005

 SAGE Publications Ltd
1 Oliver's Yard
55 City Road
London EC1Y 1SP

SAGE Publications Inc.
2455 Teller Road
Thousand Oaks, California 91320

SAGE Publications India Pvt Ltd
B-42, Panchsheel Enclave
Post Box 4109
New Delhi 110 017

British Library Cataloguing in Publication data

A catalogue record for this book is available
from the British Library

ISBN 0 7619 4232 7 (Boxed set)

Library of Congress control number available

Typeset by C&M Digitals (P) Ltd, Chennai, India
Printed in Great Britain by Cromwell Press Ltd, Trowbridge, Wiltshire

Contents

Acknowledgements

Books such as these are, inevitably, the product of the labours, wisdom and expertise of a cast of actors that would rival that of a Hollywood epic.

Our biggest thanks go to our publishers, Sage, and especially Julia Hall and Jamilah Ahmed for unswerving enthusiastic support from the very beginning and for their careful and constructive advice throughout.

We would like to thank the authors of *Publishing in Refereed Academic Journals: A Pocket Guide* and especially Miranda Hughs for her hard work and insights which led the way conceptually.

Many people reviewed the initial proposal for the *Academic's Support Kit* at Sage's request and gave it a very supportive reception. We are grateful for their early faith in us and promise to use them as referees again!

The annotated Further Reading was excellently crafted by Penny Jane Burke, Geeta Lakshmi and Simon Robb. In addition, Elizabeth Bullen gave enormous help on issues of research funding and William Spurlin helped us unravel the complexities of US universities. All are valued friends and colleagues and we appreciate their efforts.

Much of the material in the *Kit* was 'road-tested' in sessions for our postgraduate students, colleagues and others. Many other people kindly gave their time to read and comment on drafts. We are very grateful to these human guinea pigs for their hard work and can assure our readers that, as far as we are aware, none of them was harmed in the experiment.

Chris Staff of the University of Malta devised the title the *Academic's Support Kit*, and he and Brenda Murphy provided glorious Mediterranean conditions in which to write. Malmesbury, Morwell and Gozo were splendid writing localities, although Dox 'added value' at Malmesbury with his soothing yet sonorous snoring.

We are grateful to our universities – Cardiff, Monash, South Australia and the West of England – for the material support and encouragement they gave the project.

Many people in many different universities around the world inspired the books and unwittingly provided the material for our vignettes. They are too many to mention by name and besides we have had to tell their stories under other names. We are deeply indebted to our colleagues, ex-colleagues, friends, enemies, students and past students, old lovers, past and present combatants and allies and all the managers that we have ever worked with for being such a rich source of illustration and inspiration!

We particularly thank that small and select band of people who have acted as a constant source of succour and support, wise guidance and true friendship at various crucial stages of our careers: Michael Apple, Richard Johnson, Diana Leonard, Alison Mackinnon, Fazal Rizvi, Gaby Weiner, Roger Williams and Sue Willis.

Finally, as ever, our greatest thanks go to our nearest and dearest, without whose tolerance, love and hard work these books would not be in your hands today.

D.E.
J.K.
R.B.

Introducing the *Academic's Support Kit*

Before you really get into this book, you might like to know a bit more about the authors.

Rebecca Boden, from England, is professor of accounting at the University of the West of England. She did her PhD in politics immediately after graduating from her first degree (which was in history and politics). She worked as a contract researcher in a university before the shortage of academic jobs in 1980s Britain forced her into the civil service as a tax inspector. She subsequently launched herself on to the unsuspecting world of business schools as an accounting academic.

Debbie Epstein, a South African, is a professor in the School of Social Sciences at Cardiff University. She did her first degree in history and then worked briefly as a research assistant on the philosopher Jeremy Bentham's papers. Unable to read his handwriting, she went on to teach children in a variety of schools for seventeen years. She returned to university to start her PhD in her forties and has been an academic ever since.

Jane Kenway, an Australian, is professor of education at Monash University with particular responsibility for developing the field of global cultural studies in education. She was a schoolteacher and outrageous hedonist before she became an academic. But since becoming an academic she has also become a workaholic, which has done wonders for her social life, because, fortunately, all her friends are similarly inclined. Nonetheless she is interested in helping next-generation academics to be differently pleasured with regard to their work and their lives.

As you can see, we have all had chequered careers which are far from the stereotype of the lifelong academic but that are actually fairly typical. What we have all had to do is to retread ourselves, acquire new skills and learn to cope in very different environments. In our current jobs we all spend a lot of time helping and supporting people who are learning to be or developing themselves as academics. Being an accountant, Rebecca felt that there had to be a much more efficient way of helping people to get the support they need than one-to-one conversations. This book and the other five in the *Academic's Support Kit* are for all these people, and for their mentors and advisers.

We have tried to write in an accessible and friendly style. The books contain the kind of advice that we have frequently proffered our research students and colleagues, often over a cup of coffee or a meal. We suggest that you consume their contents in a similar ambience: read the whole thing through in a relaxed way first and then dip into it where and when you feel the need.

Throughout the *ASK* books we tell the stories of anonymised individuals drawn from real life to illustrate how the particular points we are making might be experienced. While you may not see a precise picture of yourself, we hope that you will be able to identify things that you have in common with one or more of our characters to help you see how you might use the book.

Pragmatic principles/principled pragmatism

In writing these books, as in all our other work, we share a number of common perceptions and beliefs.

1. Globally, universities are reliant on public funding. Downward pressure on public expenditure means that universities' financial resources are tightly squeezed. Consequently mantras such as 'budgeting', 'cost cutting', 'accountability' and 'performance indicators' have become ubiquitous, powerful drivers of institutional behaviour and academic work.

2. As a result, universities are run as corporate enterprises selling education and research knowledge. They need 'management', which is essential to running a complex organisation such as a university, as distinct from 'managerialism' – the attempted application of 'scientific management techniques' borrowed from, though often discarded by, industry and commerce. What marks managerialism out from good management is the belief that there is a one-size-fits-all suite of management solutions that can be applied to any organisation. This can lead to a situation in which research and teaching, the *raison d'etre* of universities, take second place to managerialist fads, initiatives, strategic plans, performance

indicators and so on. Thus the management tail may wag the university dog, with the imperatives of managerialism conflicting with those of academics, who usually just want to research and teach well.

3. Increasingly, universities are divided into two cultures with conflicting sets of values. On the one hand there are managerialist doctrines; on the other are more traditional notions of education, scholarship and research. But these two cultures do not map neatly on to the two job groups of 'managers' and 'academics'. Many managers in universities hold educational and scholarly values dear and fight for them in and beyond their institutions. By the same token, some academics are thoroughly and unreservedly managerialist in their approach.

4. A bit like McDonald's, higher education is a global business. Like McDonald's branches, individual universities seem independent, but are surprisingly uniform in their structures, employment practices and management strategies. Academics are part of a globalised labour force and may move from country to (better paying) country.

5. Academics' intellectual recognition comes from their academic peers rather than their employing institutions. They are part of wider national and international peer networks distinct from their employing institutions and may have academic colleagues across continents as well as nearer home. The combination of the homogeneity of higher education and academics' own networks make it possible for them to develop local identities and survival strategies based on global alliances. The very fact of this globalisation makes it possible for us to write a *Kit* that is relevant to being an academic in many different countries, despite important local variations.

6. In order to thrive in a tough environment academics need a range of skills. Very often acquiring them is left to chance, made deliberately difficult or the subject of managerialist ideology. In this *Kit* our aim is to talk straight. We want to speak clearly about what some people just 'know', but others struggle to find out. Academia is a game with unwritten and written rules. We aim to write down the unwritten rules in order to help level an uneven playing field. The slope of the playing field favours 'developed' countries and, within these, more experienced academics in more prestigious institutions. Unsurprisingly, women and some ethnic groups often suffer marginalisation.

7. Most of the skills that academics need are common across social sciences and humanities. This reflects the standardisation of working practices that has accompanied the increasing managerialisation of universities, but also the growing (and welcome) tendency to work across old disciplinary divides. The *Academic's Support Kit* is meant for social scientists, those in the humanities and those in more applied or vocational fields such as education, health sciences, accounting, business and management.

8. We are all too aware that most academics have a constant feeling of either drowning in work or running ahead of a fire or both. Indeed, we often share these feelings. Nevertheless, we think that there *are* ways of being an academic that are potentially less stressful and more personally rewarding. Academics need to find ways of playing the game in ethical and professional ways and winning. We do not advise you to accept unreasonable demands supinely. Instead, we are looking for strategies that help people retain their integrity, the ability to produce knowledge and teach well.

9. University management teams are often concerned to avoid risk. This may lead to them taking over the whole notion of 'ethical behaviour' in teaching and research and subjecting it to their own rules, which are more to do with their worries than good professional academic practice. In writing these books, we have tried to emphasise that there are richer ethical and professional ways of being in the academic world: ways of being a public intellectual, accepting your responsibilities and applying those with colleagues, students and the wider community.

And finally ...

We like the way that Colin Bundy, Principal of the School of Oriental and African Studies in London and previously Vice-Chancellor of the University of the Witwatersrand in Johannesburg, so pithily describes the differences and similarities between universities in such very different parts of the world. Interviewed for the *Times Higher Education Supplement* (27 January 2004) by John Crace, he explains:

> The difference is one of nuance. In South Africa, universities had become too much of an ivory tower and needed a reintroduction to

the pressures of the real world. In the UK, we have perhaps gone too far down the line of seeing universities as pit-stops for national economies. It's partly a response to thirty years of underfunding: universities have had to adopt the neo-utilitarian line of asserting their usefulness to justify more money. But we run the risk of losing sight of some of our other important functions. We should not just be a mirror to society, but a critical lens: we have a far more important role to play in democracy and the body politic than merely turning out graduates for the job market.

Our hope is that the *Academic's Support Kit* will help its readers develop the kind of approach exemplified by Bundy – playing in the real world but always in a principled manner.

Books in the *Academic's Support Kit*

The *Kit* comprises six books. There is no strict order in which they should be read, but this one is probably as good as any – except that you might read *Building your Academic Career* both first and last.

Building your Academic Career encourages you to take a proactive approach to getting what you want out of academic work whilst being a good colleague. We discuss the advantages and disadvantages of such a career, the routes in and the various elements that shape current academic working lives. In the second half of the book we deal in considerable detail with how to write a really good CV (résumé) and how best to approach securing an academic job or promotion.

Getting Started on Research is for people in the earlier stages of development as a researcher. In contrast to the many books available on techniques of data collection and analysis, this volume deals with the many other practical considerations around actually doing research – such as good ways to frame research questions, how to plan research projects effectively and how to undertake the various necessary tasks.

Writing for Publication deals with a number of generic issues around academic writing (including intellectual property rights) and then considers writing refereed journal articles, books and book chapters in detail as well as other, less common, forms of publication for academics. The aim is to demystify the process and to help you to become a confident, competent, successful and published writer.

Teaching and Supervision looks at issues you may face both in teaching undergraduates and in the supervision of graduate research students. This book is not a pedagogical instruction manual – there are plenty of those around, good and bad. Rather, the focus is on presenting explanations and possible strategies designed to make your teaching and supervision work less burdensome, more rewarding (for you and your students) and manageable.

Winning and Managing Research Funding explains how generic university research funding mechanisms work so that you will be better equipped to navigate your way through the financial maze associated with various funding sources. The pressure to win funding to do research is felt by nearly all academics worldwide. This book details strategies that you might adopt to get your research projects funded. It also explains how to manage your research projects once they are funded.

Building Networks addresses perhaps the most slippery of topics, but also one of the most fundamental. Despite the frequent isolation of academic work, it is done in the context of complex, multi-layered global, national, regional and local teaching or research networks. Having good networks is key to achieving what you want in academia. This book describes the kinds of networks that you might build across a range of settings, talks about the pros and cons and gives practical guidance on networking activities.

1 Who should Use this Book and How?

This book will help you get going in the business of writing and to develop your writing skill further. It will also help you tackle the complex and sometimes bewildering processes involved in getting your research published in a variety of formats.

If this is the first book in the *Academic's Support Kit* that you are reading, then you may find it useful to read 'Introducing the *Academic's Support Kit*'. Logically, if you are a beginning researcher you would be reading this book after *Getting Started on Research*. That said, it is never too soon to start thinking about and undertaking writing projects. If you have already read *Getting Started on Research* you will know that writing is an integral and on-going part of the research process which starts with your proposal and never comes to an end.

This book will be especially useful for you if you are:

- A research student who has yet to write for publication.
- Someone who has had an academic job for a while, but who has not yet got going with writing and publishing their research.
- Someone in their first academic job (with or without a research degree) who needs to acquire writing and publication skills.
- A more experienced academic who is mentoring someone in one or more of these categories.

You may:

- Want to overcome your anxieties about your writing and publishing.
- Wish to share your ideas, theories, thoughts and research findings with others.
- Need to develop your career profile. (For more advice about how to do this, you should read *Building an Academic Career*.)
- Be required to report to your research funders about the work they have paid for.

- Be under pressure from your employing institution to publish your research work.
- Be a successful writer and publisher yourself but need to know how to help others do the same.

Looking back at this list, it's apparent that there are two explanations of why people write and publish their research. The first explanation is that writing and publication are fundamental to the process of being an academic. It is imperative for researchers to engage in academic debate and discussion and tell other people what they are doing in their own work. In short, there's very little point to researching unless you are going to be able to tell people about your work.

The second explanation is to do with institutional pressures on and controls over academic work. Managers like to manage what they can measure, and publication represents a tangible and supposedly measurable output of the process of thinking and intellectual work. It is, therefore, easy to see why publication has become a yardstick for institutions and their funders. We think it's really important that academics do publish, but when the measurement of publication (either by volume, perceived quality or use by others) becomes a management tool, it can generate perverse incentives that distort the real intellectual value of the publication process. In short, the tail starts wagging the dog.

Publication can be used as quite a strict management tool, so be aware that you are very likely to come under these sorts of pressures. This is a great shame, because we think that writing and publication for what we regard as the 'right' academic reasons should be one of the most fun and rewarding aspects of being an academic. Consider the story below of how a group of academics lost their jobs because of their perceived failure to publish enough.

It all adds up to a pretty Brum do

In theory, things couldn't look brighter for higher education: a government commitment to increase student numbers by 2010; superb research assessment exercise scores in 2001; a 'demonstrable improvement' in teaching quality; and an acknowledgement by the Higher Education Funding Council for England that there will have ▶

▶ to be a net rise of between 15,000 and 17,000 academic staff in universities by 2010.

But a harsh reality belies this picture. Of late, there have been wholesale departmental closures, cost-cutting regimes, widespread redundancies and bottom-lines slipping badly into the red.

Academics need to pay attention to what is happening in their own backyards before it is too late. The closure of the department of cultural studies and sociology at Birmingham University is a perfect case study.

Cultural studies at Birmingham has been the single most inter-nationally influential academic group in the creation and development of the discipline. It achieved a perfect 24 in its last teaching quality assessment, student demand was buoyant and it was financially sound.

In the 2001 RAE, [Research Assessment Exercise] its entry was changed, without consultation, by senior managers with no expertise in the discipline. The head of department protested, predicting that this would damage the score. The result was a grading of 3a. Management decided that no score of less than 4 could be tolerated and moved to 'restructure' the department. All staff have taken what is technically voluntary severance, under conditions they maintain amount to duress.

This story tells us four things. First, it demonstrates a massive divergence between the world of academics and the management elite. The work of academics achieves and sustains the reputation of an institution, while managers, driven by different norms and values, have the power of life or death. Thus, the global academic outcry against the closure has fallen on the cloth ears of managers dedicated to the crudest forms of 'rational management'.

Second, it shows the power of pseudo-objective exercises such as the RAE. Staff were judged on the basis of a submission not of their own writing, under a research assessment regime not of their making, and were deemed to have 'failed'. The objectivity of the RAE gave management's judgements apparently greater legitimacy and authority than the outcry of academics worldwide.

Third, it demonstrates the extent to which managers fail to think strategically or in a businesslike way. The next RAE will take place in 2008 (not 2006 as Birmingham anticipated) under a scheme yet to be determined by Sir Gareth Roberts' review. Birmingham's managers have made short-term decisions based on the expectation of the ▶

▶ continued application of a research assessment system that they already know to be defunct.

Further, the department represented an important 'brand', crucial to attracting students, especially foreign ones, and staff. That brand has now been destroyed.

Fourth, the plight of the former staff exemplifies the disciplinary nature of the relationship between management and academics. Academics are subject to many different performance audit regimes, and management can choose arbitrarily which to act on. In this case, management used a 'failure' when it suited them, while ignoring concurrent audit 'successes'. Research and pedagogic success, in academics' terms and those of management, continues to go unrewarded while failure, as determined by management, is brutally punished.

Such an analysis will have little comfort for those who have lost their jobs and for Birmingham's academic community. The rest of us ignore the lessons at our peril.

(Rebecca Boden and Debbie Epstein, *Times Higher Education Supplement*, 20 September 2002)

Remember that writing and publication are important academic activities that bring real rewards. There is little more satisfying than getting your first article or book published and feeling that you have produced something of real value. The secret is to learn to get what you need out of the activity in order to work well as a professional and enjoy yourself, whilst managing and balancing the adverse (and sometimes perverse) institutional pressures. This book is meant to help you achieve that balance.

Before going on, we'd like to introduce some characters who might benefit from reading this book.

Jonny has been an academic for a number of years. His institution made a shift to becoming research-led and he decided to become a researcher. He registered for a part-time PhD in history. When he was ▶

▶ planning his PhD, aware of institutional pressures to publish (and the career benefits of so doing), he designed his thesis so that he could publish papers on aspects of his work as he went along. He ended up writing papers in tandem with particular chapters of his thesis. He struggled with the first paper – he had excellent data but found difficulty in shaping it into an argument for an article. He got three professors in his department and his supervisor/adviser to help him to restructure his writing. When everyone was happy that the paper was in good shape, he submitted it to a prestigious journal and it was accepted with only minor revisions. He was absolutely delighted when his paper was accepted and got promoted shortly afterwards. He is now writing a second paper in tandem with the next chapter of his thesis.

Claudia has become an academic as a second career. She was not well advised about her writing and publication in the first few years of her academic job and, as a result, had no publications to contribute when her department's research output was audited. Her confidence was severely damaged by this experience and she seriously considered giving up her academic career. Rather than do that, she worked hard with her newly acquired mentor to develop some of her existing work for presentation at a small, friendly conference and subsequent publication in a refereed journal. Her success in this regard boosted her confidence sufficiently that she decided to begin her PhD, with her mentor as her supervisor. She is now working on a second paper.

Bina has a first-class degree in mathematics. She subsequently became a schoolteacher and undertook an MA in the Sociology of Education, which required her to begin to think and write sociologically instead of mathematically. She is now becoming a confident writer although she originally thought that she would never be able to write sociology (rather than maths). She has a couple of publications to her credit and is thinking about how to develop her writing and publication profile.

2 The Business of Writing

In this chapter we address a number of generic issues around the business of writing, before moving on in subsequent chapters to discuss specific writing forms and publication formats.

Read this!

Like small children, before you can write you have to be able to read – and, in your case, read research. Good reading habits are helpful in two ways. First, writing and publishing can be thought of as joining in an academic discussion, albeit a written one at a slow speed. Unless you are abreast of what others are saying, you won't know what constitutes a valuable, valid and interesting intervention by you. Second, like any other skill, writing is one that you have to learn and keep developing. By critically reading others' work you should be able to learn what works well and what doesn't.

Your reading needs to be systematic and rigorous. If you are developing good research skills it is highly likely that you will have begun to develop good reading skills, as you can't have the first without the second. Some people with good scholarship practices will already have good reading skills, but will not necessarily be undertaking their own research.

Handy hints for effective reading

Even though you may already have good reading habits, we thought it worthwhile recapping here the things about reading that help with writing.

1. Get the habit

All academics have really busy lives. Stuff like regular reading of things that will augment your basic knowledge base (as opposed to reading things you have to) often slips off the edge of our mental in-trays. Try to avoid relegating this activity to those non-existent periods when you 'have time' by building a regular reading slot into every working day or, at least, into every working week. This is far from easy, and you may have to be determined and ingenious to achieve it. If you have a long commute to work using public transport or have to hang around while your kids are at piano lessons, use the time to read. Our experience is that if you intend to do your academic reading at bedtime then it just doesn't happen – you fall asleep before you have finished the first page.

2. Read actively, not passively

It is treacherously easy to believe that you are really reading when in actual fact you aren't. Your eyes go over the words but by the end of the chapter you have forgotten the beginning of it because you read it as if you were reading a novel. When you read academic work, you need to engage actively with the material by interrogating it. Ask yourself questions as you go along. Do I really agree with this? How convincing is this argument? What holes can I pick in that one? What would I say to the author if they were explaining their ideas to me in person? How can I make use of these ideas or data to inform my own? What key concepts is the author working with and why? If you read actively in this way, your reading will be of positive benefit in keeping up with the development of knowledge in your particular field.

Reading done properly is very time-consuming. We think it is a good idea to avoid redundant reading by quickly skimming through a text first of all, checking that it is what you expect and likely to be of use to you. In journal articles the abstract at the beginning (and often available on-line on the publishers' Web pages) is there specifically to help you decide whether or not you want to read the whole thing in depth. With books, use the contents page and the index intelligently to decide whether to read the book or not. It never ceases to amaze us how many students we come across who have absolutely no notion of the existence of indexes, let alone how they might be used. We harbour the suspicion that many of these students eventually become academics with the same lacunae of knowledge. Reading the introduction quickly, especially of an edited collection where the editor discusses the contents and draws them together, can also help.

Once you have skimmed a text, don't think that you've actually read it. Skimming enables you to make a decision about whether to invest the time in detailed and proper reading. Unfortunately, we have discovered that there is no natural osmosis from text to head, either by leaving books on your shelf for months or years or placing them under your pillow at night. There is really no substitute for actually reading.

Good writers usually devote significant effort to structuring their writing carefully and leaving plenty of signposts for the reader, to let them know how the structure of the piece works. It is a foolish reader who ignores this thoughtful help. Use sections and signposts to divide up your reading and note-taking efforts and to make explicit to yourself what the structure of the argument is. This may be particularly important when you are reading complex or difficult pieces in which you encounter new and challenging ideas. Debbie tries to summarise each section in such pieces with the text closed after she has finished reading it. Rebecca works out what each paragraph is saying and makes a note of that as she goes along. Jane heavily marks the bits of interest and indicates in the margins how they link with her current research or teaching, returning to these later to write notes on the links. If you can write your own abstract of someone else's article or chapter when you get to the end of reading it, you can be pretty sure that you have read it thoroughly and intelligently and will not forget what it says. That means you will be able to use it in future without having to reread it several times.

3. Read widely

All too often, people maintain that there is nothing for them to read in their particular closely focused area of research. They almost believe that because no-one has written about their particular topic they are excused from reading. In fact, good researchers and writers read widely and eclectically, often drawing ideas from unexpected places or disciplines. If you read actively, you should be constantly asking yourself, 'How might these ideas or concepts be used in my writing?'

Victoria is a PhD student looking at the role of architecture in the employment treatment of visually impaired people. She was somewhat alarmed when she started to discover, unsurprisingly, that ▶

there was no literature on architecture and blindness. In doing her research training, she was required to write an assessed course paper critiquing the literature in her research area. Her supervisor advised her to look in the extensive sociological, cultural studies and social policy literatures on disability. In that literature Victoria found well developed theoretical work on the construction of disability as a social concept and on disabled identities. In her own work she was able to successfully deploy these concepts and theories in examining the role of architecture in this area.

Emily is at the beginning of her PhD. She is interested in how boys from different social classes learn to ride horses, often in environments dominated by girls, and the issues faced by those who continue after puberty and become equestrian professionals. However, there is nothing written that draws together the questions of masculinities, social class and riding. Emily is drawing on the extensive literatures on masculinity, class and embodiment to frame her own research.

4. Be a style guru

In reading actively, don't just concentrate on the academic content and argument. Develop a keen critical eye, or rather ear, for the different genres of academic writing. Recognise elliptical and obscure prose for what it is and stop yourself from slipping into a similar trap. Learn from others how to express complex and difficult ideas in clear, albeit sophisticated, ways. Learn to distinguish between academic writing that is necessarily complex and therefore difficult to read and that which is just plain showing-off or sloppiness. Just as you wouldn't expect a motor mechanic to talk about a car engine without using technical terms for its constituent parts, so academic disciplines have their own particular languages that you must learn and use sensibly.

Develop a keen eye for what a well structured piece of writing looks like. Most disciplines have tacit writing formats and you need to learn how these work in your discipline and how to deploy them. Above all, use your reading to learn about style, language and formats in your field and to think about how you will develop your own distinctive version of these. Find authors whose writing moves, inspires and stimulates you and analyse what's good about it. Learn your lessons from that.

5. Take note!

Your reading will be far more productive and yield longer-term benefits if you keep good notes both of what you have read and what's in it.

Make a careful record of the bibliographic details of your reading sufficient for you to cite the material in anything that you write, thus saving you time. It will also let you find the material again if you don't have your own copy. In *Getting Started on Research* we discuss bibliographic software packages that will help you do this very efficiently.

Keep systematic notes. Avoid, at all costs, extensive detail and exact copying of whole paragraphs. Everyone has their own system of note taking and you have to do what suits you best. You might:

- Use the note function on a bibliographic software package.
- Make notes in your research notebooks.
- Staple pieces of paper to the front of copies of articles.
- Have virtual conversations by writing in the margins of your books – but never anybody else's, especially those borrowed from a library.
- Draw a diagram or mind map representing the shape of the arguments.

Whatever system you adopt, make sure that you get the author's argument right in your notes or you run the risk of misrepresentation in your own writing.

You might like to think about making notes on:

- The main lines of the argument.
- Interesting empirical evidence.
- Important 'facts'.
- Your own reactions to the argument or the data.
- The theories and methods employed.
- The relevance to the particular thing you are writing/researching at present.
- Page references for particular parts of the argument or quotes that you might want to come back to.
- Connections with the writings of other authors you have read.

Quotable quotes

In your reading you will come across interesting snippets of writing that really encapsulate something important that you want to engage with. In such cases, copy a brief section exactly to incorporate into your own writing. Always make a clear note that this text is copied and keep a careful record of exactly where (including page or paragraph numbers) it is from. In copying out quotes, preserve the original spelling and be careful, especially when using the spell checker, not to alter it from the original. Even quite well established academics sometimes fail to do this and can suffer serious consequences as a result. Remember, plagiarism is the most serious and least forgivable of academic sins.

Get writing!

Psychological issues

Committing yourself to paper can be an intimidating process, particularly if you haven't done it for a long time. The benefit of writing is that it lets others see our work and enables them to engage with and challenge it. You can mitigate the entirely understandable feeling of exposure and vulnerability this often engenders by doing your research and writing well – that way it will stand up to scrutiny.

Novice researchers often delay writing or get uptight about it because, very wrongly, they perceive that others find it easy and they find it difficult. Writing does get easier with practice, but it is always hard work and even the most experienced of writers have bad days in which they write one paragraph and then find a host of other work avoidance strategies. Anyone who says that they find writing easy may simply be trying to undermine your confidence. Because it is hard, don't be ashamed about having to ask for help. There is no virtue in struggling on your own if there are people who can help you out.

If you are worried about starting writing and keep putting it off, practise just getting words down on paper or up on the screen. As we have said elsewhere in this *Kit*: 'Don't get it right, get it written' – well, at least in the first instance. The more you practise, the better you will get. So try to write something each day, perhaps in your research journal. As time goes on, you will become more accomplished and comfortable with the writing process.

If you can overcome these wholly understandable psychological barriers, you should find writing exciting and enjoyable. A well crafted piece of writing will give you a real sense of personal achievement and satisfaction.

When do I start?

Some people imagine a magic land in which researchers know everything, have all of their material and data assembled, everything neatly organised and to hand, all their arguments marshalled and rehearsed and are ready to simply 'write up'. We have never been there and treat individuals who claim they have with the same scepticism as we treat people who claim to have been abducted by aliens. There is no point at which writing becomes a simple and straightforward task of 'writing up'. The process of writing is much more complex, messy and creative than that.

The perfect conditions in which you are 'ready to write' do not exist. Writing is an on-going and iterative process. As such, it helps you sort out your ideas, and shapes and guides your research in an iterative way. Additionally, constant writing helps you to develop and hone your writing skills.

We cannot overstress the need to write early and write often. Because writing is a learned skill and an activity that is integral to the research process, your writing should start at the same time as your research. Your early efforts may be:

- A few paragraphs in which you contest or explore what you have been reading.
- Fieldwork notes written up in a discursive/analytical way.
- A formal literature review in which you evaluate and synthesise your reading.
- A vignette from your fieldwork.
- A formal exposition of your research questions or an 'autobiography of the question'.
- A formal research proposal (for your own use or to submit to get funding).

Whilst none of this needs to be long, you should approach it in exactly the same sort of way that you would writing for publication. That is, use these writing exercises as a way of learning writing skills as well as helping you in your research. If you work in this way, these pieces of writing will eventually feed into the construction of pieces for publication. We are great believers in recycling: words written down are rarely wasted.

Planning your writing

It is surprising how many people begin to write before having made a plan. The principal reason why you need to plan is that it will:

- Ensure clarity about the questions/issues to be addressed.
- Make sure that you know, at least in outline form, what argument you are trying to make.
- Outline the data that will support your argument.
- Ensure that you don't leave anything important out and, equally, help you see which bits of your knowledge you can leave out of this particular piece.
- Ensure that you are telling a coherent story and that your writing has a viable structure.
- Stop you from simply writing down everything you know and ever wanted to know about the subject.
- Focus your thoughts and subsequent writing.

The clarity of purpose and structure that a plan will help you develop will be reflected in your writing. It follows that planning is an active and creative process. Plans don't just spring fully formed from people's heads. They are pieces of work in their own right that constitute an important part of the research and writing processes. As such, it may take a great deal of time and effort to get a plan right, but doing so saves time later and makes your subsequent work easier.

That said, it's a poor plan that can't be modified. Few people can write exactly to the original plan. As part of the writing process, your ideas, arguments and questions will evolve and become clearer as you write. Indeed, some people say that they don't know what they think until they've written it. They don't mean they haven't planned, only that the specifics and clarity of their arguments emerge in the writing process.

Everyone has their own way of planning their writing. Here are several that the three of us regularly use. Which one we choose will depend on the purposes of the writing, the difficulty of the particular piece, whom we are writing with and for.

- Talk your ideas through with your co-authors, peers, mentors or advisers. Sometimes people find it helpful to use a whiteboard or flip chart to make notes and draw diagrams as they talk.
- Rebecca keeps a special box of coloured gel pens and pencils and likes to draw multicoloured mind maps on large pieces of paper. Sometimes she tapes paper together as her ideas burgeon or uses large sheets of children's drawing paper.
- Some people of an artistic bent like to draw 'rich pictures' to visualise their ideas.
- Debbie likes to think about what she wants to write for a long time, letting ideas mature in her head before putting 'pen to paper'. Ideally, she likes to have virtually written the paper in her head before more formal planning and writing begin.
- Writing an abstract can be a great way of giving yourself a route map for the paper you will write. A one-page abstract forces you to present a coherent story about your intended writing. Some people use headings and bullet points to create their plans.
- One technique, which is particularly useful for complex writing, is to draw a vertical line down the middle of your page. On the left-hand side write the points of the argument in their logical order and on the right fill in the evidence (literature or your empirical data) that you will use to support your argument.
- A variation of this is to write the main points of the argument on index cards, with the supporting evidence on the back. Play around with arranging the order of the cards on a big table or the floor (beware disruptive toddlers and dogs) until you work out what makes a coherent and logical argument.
- Jane tends to write out the skeleton of the argument after lots of thinking, reading, looking at her data and general anguish. Then she weaves her theory and her data though the skeleton.

The architecture of writing

Buildings usually contain a variety of materials: bricks, glass, concrete, etc. In the same way academic writing has to consist of different elements. Unless you are writing in some of the less conventional genres, which we will discuss shortly, these elements should include:

- A question, or questions, being addressed.
- An overarching argument that contains different strands and themes.
- Evidence to support the argument, which may consist of empirical data collected from archives or fieldwork, or it might consist of the writings of others. Most likely, it will include both.

Just as a pile of bricks, glass and concrete does not a building make, so a poorly constructed pile of questions, arguments and evidence does not constitute a convincing and powerful piece of academic writing. Academic writing, like buildings, needs to be put together in a precise and skilled fashion. As we've said, a plan is an essential first step in such a construction exercise. Builders don't just start randomly arranging bricks and carry on until they find something that looks interesting.

You must not make your reader do more work than is absolutely necessary. Be kind to them by giving them signposts, explaining what you are doing, using clear language and pointing to the significance of what you are saying. If you do all this, the reader is more likely not only to get real value from your writing, but also to read it in the first place. It's only when you are an academic mega-star (and sometimes not even then) that readers will persist with impenetrable and poorly written texts in order to uncover the meaning.

Our best and most basic advice on structure is that which we give to undergraduate students:

- Say what you are going to say.
- Say it.
- Say what you've said.

By 'say what you're going to say' we mean that near the start of your writing you should introduce what the focus of your enquiry or discussion is (that is, your question or issues) and explain what your general line of argument and sources of evidence will be. You also need to set out the order in which you will approach things. However, it's important not to pre-empt your argument. Rather, use this section as a way of enticing the reader to go further. Of course there is no need to be unduly ponderous about it.

Many academics approach the introductory section of their papers in much the same way. Usually such a section will consist of the following elements, in this order:

- An opening story, vignette, event or quote that the reader can instantly connect with from their everyday or professional experience. This is designed to capture the reader's attention and make them start to look at the world around them with a deeper interest and desire for understanding. An excellent example of the use of this device is the first few pages of Foucault's *Discipline and Punish* (1977), in which he describes, in gory detail, the brutal execution of Damiens, the regicide. If you have a strong stomach, by the end of this description you will be hooked and will read the rest of the book. This works as an opening because of the immediate and disturbing effect of the description on your emotions as a reader.

- You can then use the opening to frame the questions or issues that will form the focus of the writing. You might say, 'That's very interesting. What questions or issues can we frame around this that will enable us to develop knowledgeable insights into what is going on here?' This helps the reader to see that you are not just writing the paper because no-one has written a paper on the topic before. You are emphasising that you have a focus and that you really are trying to explore or discuss a worthwhile issue or question.

- You can then set out the sort of arguments and evidence that will be used to address the questions and/or issues. Be careful not to go into too much detail here – you just have to say enough to give the reader clear signposts about what is coming and what the overall shape of the argument will be.

- Finally, conclude this section by setting out the structure of the rest of the paper. You should divide your paper into logical sections, each one doing a particular task. You need to flag up to the reader how many sections are coming, what each does and how they fit together to form a coherent whole.

Once you have set out what you are going to say in your introduction, you can move to 'saying it' in one or more subsequent sections (in a paper) or chapters (in a book). What these are will vary according to your discipline and the sort of argument that you are making. They may well include (in varying orders) a discussion of the public story so far from the available literature, the introduction/discussion of various concepts or theories that you intend to deploy, some specific empirical data and a discursive analysis of data. You might organise your substantive arguments thematically. You might start with the general and move to the specific or vice versa. There are many ways to slice the loaf. However you break up what you are saying, make sure that the divisions are logical, that the links between them are made and that the overall writing is coherent and consistent.

Your ultimate aim is to give the reader a sense of being carefully led through your thoughts and arguments. With a building, an architect will make sure that there aren't any floors or windows missing and that there are no extraneous bits dangling off the sides that are neither use nor ornament. Do the same with your writing. If you have interesting things to say that don't fit in with the general run of this piece of writing, save them for a later piece. You can't make something not worth saying into a good piece of writing by throwing in extra bits to adorn it.

When you have had your say, there comes a time near the end of the paper in which you need to say what you have said. Don't repeat yourself here. The aim is to summarise your arguments, your data and what you have demonstrated or contributed to knowledge. Use this section to emphasise the value of your message and perhaps to indicate where further work might usefully be done. At this stage it is especially important to have an authoritative voice – if your research is good, then confidence is justified.

If you follow these three simple stages you will have a clear structure or architecture to your writing. Be kind to your reader and make it explicit when you are moving to a different stage of your writing by using headings and sub-headings. These act as signposts, effectively saying, 'Something different is happening now.' But don't use too many headings and subheadings and sub-subheadings because this makes your writing feel cluttered and ruins the flow.

Speak up!

Inexperienced authors often find it difficult to find their own authorial voice. This manifests itself in a number of ways.

- Some writers make extensive use of phrases like 'it may be the case that' or 'perhaps' or 'it could be argued' and so on. Whilst we would urge you to avoid making unsupported assertions in your writing, be confident about the validity of your evidence and arguments. If you really are in doubt then you shouldn't be using them. We think, as others have argued, that, on balance, it may, in the main, be best to avoid statements that might, perhaps, appear to others to be, er, somewhat tentative.

- Some writing is heavily 'sandbagged': someone has gone through it with the 'reference pepperpot', liberally sprinkling references everywhere as a pathetic means of attempting to legitimise what is being said (Blair, 2119; Forbes, 2110; Jones, 2230; Lee, 2112; Mbeki, 2115; Patel, 2120; Smith, 2117; Thatcher, 2118; Wilson, 2110). It is, of course essential to acknowledge the work of others properly where you have drawn on it. However, it is not necessary to give a list of ten references at every turn of your argument. Such practices are either a sign of low confidence or a way of showing off how much you have read. Note, however, that doctoral theses are a different genre and it may be necessary to reference more heavily to demonstrate that you have done all the reading that your examiners might deem requisite.

- Other writing relies heavily on extensive quotes from the works of others. Our advice to budding authors is to use quotations in only two situations. First, you may be undertaking a detailed textual analysis of the passage, engaging specifically with it. And second, you have made your own point and may then use a quotation to illustrate or emphasise what you have said. The latter should be used sparingly.

'NEVER USE A QUOTE TO MAKE YOUR OWN POINT' (Brown, 2010: 971; see also Jones, 2023; Li, 2027; Smith, 2120; Mphaphlele, 2017; Patel, 2035).

- Sometimes, the language used is deliberately obscure and obfuscatory in an attempt to make the author sound 'academic'. Symbolically exclusionary textual devices may be used elliptically as connotative of the author's dominance in hegemonic discourse, lending legitimacy to epistemologically dubious and ontologically unconvincing arguments, which may themselves be derivative, reductionist and essentialist.

- Often, novice writers are concerned about whether they are allowed to use the 'first person' in their writing. This varies across disciplines and you will have to take advice. However, the present authors would argue that the use of the third person is a way of distancing oneself from what is being said and not taking responsibility for it. Epstein, Kenway and Boden also argue convincingly that the use of the third person may create a false and unsustainable sense of objectivity in the text.

In the end, everyone has to find their own distinctive voice. The best writers can often be recognised immediately by their style.

Playing to the audience

Never forget that you are writing for your readers. Help them and don't make them work harder than they have to. Keep in mind your target audience as you write and be conscious of constructing your argument and using language which speaks to those people directly. When Debbie started her academic career, she always tried to write for the curious and enquiring teacher that she had been a few years earlier. If you are too ambitious and imagine that your typical audience will be international academic superstars, then you will be unduly inhibited. In writing this *Kit* we have always tried to hold in our heads an image of what sort of person you, the reader, are: what sort of job you are doing, what countries you are working in, how you might be feeling about various issues and what sort of phraseology you will relate to.

The further you move away from actually being the person you are writing for, the harder it becomes to remember how to write for them. For this reason, it is a good idea to get friends and acquaintances in your target groups to read your drafts before you attempt to publish them.

We are not saying that you should always pander to the base desires of lazy readers. Whilst you have to think about what your reader needs or wants (and the two aren't always the same) from your writing, this does not exonerate you from the responsibility of remaining true to your own work or challenging their preconceptions, prejudices or unthinking assumptions. But they won't respond to your challenges unless you can engage them, make them want to read you and persist in trying to 'get' what you are saying.

The ultimate aim is to make your audience want to sit up and listen to you. So you need to inveigle, seduce, titillate, enthral, enchant, fascinate and leave them a metaphorical trail of breadcrumbs through the forest so that they feel secure about where they are going and how to get back. You also want to challenge, enrage (and engage), question, disturb and excite them.

Generically speaking

Academics write about their research in a number of quite distinctive genres. Later in this book we explain in more detail how to publish your work in some of the most common forms. In this section we want to get you to think about the gamut of writing genres that you might engage in. The main ones are:

- Dissertations and theses, which can be seen as 'apprentice pieces' for novice researchers.
- Academic journal articles.
- Book chapters in collections, usually edited by other academics.
- Books for academic audiences, often called research monographs.
- Books about research findings for practitioners and policy makers (that is, the 'end users' of research).
- Popular books based on research but written for non-academic audiences.
- Professional journal articles.
- Reports for specific organisations and/or government departments which may or may not be widely published.
- Newspaper or other popular press pieces.
- Conference and seminar papers and posters.

In addition, some academics disseminate their research using other media such as film making or artwork, but here we are dealing only with written texts.

Each of these generic forms has its own implicit and/or explicit rules and conventions. These are determined by a *mélange* of influences such as:

- The development of shared common practices and traditions in particular disciplinary fields, subject areas or communities.
- The needs and desires of the audience.
- The requirements of publishers, editors and research funders.

We can't go into the specifics of each genre for every discipline and field of study. You have to correctly identify the genre in which you are writing and then discern the rules governing it. The best way to do this is to read several exemplars. Ask around for the best examples on which to model your own writing.

Rob was a PhD student nearing the end of his maximum registration period. Unfortunately his supervisor went on long-term sick leave and he had not previously been in the practice of writing. Without a supervisor, he took several weeks off work to 'write up' his thesis. His thesis was allowed to be a maximum of 80,000 words. Struggling along on his own, he realised that he had problems when all he could produce was 105,000 words of 'literature review'. He quickly sought help from a new supervisor, who counselled him on what a thesis should look like, helped him to plan his final text and sent him to the library to read some examples.

Jemima was commissioned by a research council to evaluate a major research programme that it had funded. As she had never done that kind of exercise before, the Economic and Social Research Council sent her three examples of similar evaluations on which she could model her own report to meet the funder's requirements successfully.

Because academics need to write for different audiences, using different genres, you will find that the same ideas or piece of research can and should be re-presented in many different formats. This gives an economy of scale to your writing, giving you multiple pay-offs.

You may wish to experiment, from time to time, with novel or innovative forms of writing. Some journals actively encourage this. Remember though that it is difficult to pull off an innovative writing style if you are an inexperienced writer. It is best to concentrate on getting the basic skills first, as getting less conventional stuff published can be problematic.

The hierarchy of which generic form is most prestigious varies across disciplines and countries. However, it is always the case in the academic world that peer-refereed articles in international academic journals or authored books published by reputable academic publishers are rated more highly than most other forms.

Challenging conventional writing

You may find yourself encouraged or required to write in a style that creates or reinforces notions of knowledge as neutral and objective. We think that such claims about the validity of knowledge are, in themselves, extremely political and subjective. Some writing styles seek to address such issues as power and authority in the way in which they are constructed. Such styles can be hard to carry off successfully, and you may have to cut your teeth on more conventional modes of writing first in order to get yourself established.

In *Publishing in Refereed Academic Journals* (Deakin University, 1998) Jane Kenway, Noel Gough and Miranda Hughs set out the following considerations to bear in mind when stretching yourself as an author. We've paraphrased them below.

- *Be aware that your research story has a personal or political dimension.* Authors often write as the neutral narrators of how they discovered 'research facts'. Yet we all bring to our writing a host of theoretical, political and cultural assumptions. These frequently remain unexamined, even by the writers themselves, and some people still struggle with the notion that their personal beliefs are relevant to or influence the knowledge that they produce. Hence the debate about the use of the first or third person.
- *Tell the research story from more than one perspective.* Think about presenting your work from a variety of perspectives or in a number of different voices. This is particularly suited to multi-authored writing, where group-work gives a rich opportunity for analysing the theoretical, cultural and political stance of each participant. If your research involved a number of respondents with very different perspectives, you could think about presenting their different angles as a kind of play script or conversation.
- *Present the research process in its honest, messy form.* As authors, we can tend to present our research as a linear story as if it really happened that way. But we all know that there are false starts and wrong tacks, or that serendipity plays a role. Your research may have failed to show the expected (or any) results, or a seminar, article or chance conversation unexpectedly crystallised a research solution. Writing about these experiences can help to challenge the belief that the truth is 'out there' waiting to be discovered, instead of the truth being something that we create ourselves.

- *Write in the contradiction.* Include the logical and theoretical contradictions, the dead-end trails of arguments. They may be aspects of your work that you find troubling (and would prefer to forget!) but you may find that others have had similar problems. It may indicate the inadequacies of a particular theoretical or methodological stance and contribute to developments in method or theory. Or it may show that neat solutions are not always possible. But, again, you must be sure that the problem lies at the theoretical or methodological level and is not due to inadequate analysis on your part.

Doing it together

Writing something entirely on your own as a sole author can be a lonely activity. However, it is one that you need to be expert and experienced in because:

- Regulations, such as when you are writing a thesis, may require it.
- You may need to demonstrate your competence beyond doubt for promotion/appointment purposes.
- Most important, there will be things that you want to say that are very particular to you and you need to give voice to.

You will therefore probably have to develop and maintain your capacity to write on your own. But writing with others can be immensely rewarding, creative and generative. It *can* also be very much more enjoyable than sole authorship, but you have to pick your co-authors carefully. If you are inexperienced, writing with others can be a good way of learning to write.

Collaborative writing is often an integral and natural part of collaborative research. If you have great data, or are a real rookie, beware the friendly but not well published colleague who offers to 'write your stuff up with you', despite not being involved in the research. They are probably more interested in getting their name on your publications than really helping you.

Claire was a junior faculty member undertaking a PhD. She had to have an appraisal meeting with her head of school. The head of school asked her what she was working on. Claire enthused about a great idea she'd had and explained that she had submitted an abstract of a ▶

▶ paper on the topic to a prestigious conference and had drafted nearly three-quarters of the paper. The head of school, with no publications ever to their name, said, 'I have come across this published paper in this area. If I give it to you, we could write your paper together.' Claire, wisely and quite rightly, politely demurred.

When writing collaboratively ensure that everyone brings something to the party. For instance, if you are the junior partner you may have done the bulk of the data collection but are reliant on more experienced colleagues to help with the analysis and the writing. You might, in contrast, be working with people who are your academic peers in terms of experience and ability where you bring different strengths and knowledges to the process of writing. The point is that the varying contributions should reflect the experience, skill and work done by all the collaborative authors (and that authorship attribution should too).

Tanya is working closely with Ivor, one of her formal mentees in her department. She was responsible for getting him started as a researcher and is providing some 'on the job' research training for him as part of a project that they are undertaking jointly. Ivor's main contribution has been undertaking the extensive fieldwork. Tanya has been treating writing as a sort of training exercise – showing Ivor how to draft and craft and then sending him off with specific tasks related to the writing that needed to be done. They will share the authorship of the papers. An eventual aim is that Ivor will feel confident and experienced enough to undertake his own writing projects.

Debbie works extensively with Richard. At the start of their research and writing collaboration Richard was significantly more senior than she was and had just examined her PhD thesis, though they are now both professors. He was initially the more experienced writer and theorist whilst she was more experienced as an ethnographer and more knowledgeable about the subject area they were exploring together. Over the years they have written together in a number of ▶

> different ways: sitting down at the keyboard and writing every sentence together; one of them drafting a chapter or paper and the other revising it; bringing ideas together and one or other of them writing the paper. Both of them feel strongly that they have learned a huge amount from each other, both substantively and about the writing process.

Pick co-authors with care. Choose people you know and trust, and if it doesn't work, don't write with them again (however much you like them), because it's not worth the grief. In contrast, you can become close friends with someone by writing with them, and particular collaborations may stay with you throughout your academic career. It's a good idea to choose someone with whom you share a theoretical, political and/or epistemological standpoint, but don't necessarily choose people who are identical to you – different knowledges can be complementary and enriching.

As with any other piece of academic work, collaborative writing needs to be planned and agreed on in advance. We speak more below about getting the attribution of authorship right, but it needs to be part of this planning and agreement stage.

There is no 'right' way of actually doing collaborative writing. You have to devise a way of working together that suits all the authors. There are a number of variations.

- Sitting together at the keyboard and deciding mutually on each word. This can be really productive and you are likely to develop a joint authorial voice that is different from either of your individual ones. The great advantage is that you can keep each other going and spark ideas off each other. The disadvantage is the difficulty of finding mutually convenient blocks of time when you can work together.
- Planning together and then one person drafting the first version for alteration/amendment by the other(s). This method often generates a productive game of drafting ping-pong as the text is bounced back and forth between authors.
- Planning together and then dividing up the writing tasks into discrete chunks and allocating them to specific authors. The skill in this method comes in uniting all the variously authored sections into

one coherent text that doesn't read like a dog's breakfast. When done well, it can be a very effective way of writing and doesn't impose the onerous responsibility of producing an entire first draft on one person. It does, however, take good editorial skills.

- In long-standing partnerships it may be that some jointly authored pieces are almost entirely written by one person, though the ideas will have been discussed extensively. This method is fine as long as the writing work is evenly distributed in the long term.

Which particular version of collaboration you choose will depend on the situation and how you get on with your collaborators. It's important to be flexible, using a number of methods, sometimes in the same teams at different times.

There are a number of potential pitfalls in collaborative writing.

- Some people write very badly and you may have to devote endless time and energy to being their sub-editor.
- Writing together is more, not less, labour-intensive.
- It's important not to let people down, and to let your co-authors know if you are not able to deliver on time.
- Sometimes you can have arguments with your co-authors over matters such as content, style, argument and authorship. You need to find a way of resolving these in a mature manner.
- If you always work with more senior colleagues, others may think that the work is theirs rather than yours.
- If it doesn't go well, for whatever reason, you risk falling out with friends and losing important relationships.

Handy hints for successful writing

Finally, we have a few quick tips to help you become successful academic writers.

1. Write more 'shortly'. That is, you should generally go for maximum clarity and conciseness in your writing style.
2. Avoid using the passive voice, where possible. It is both more wordy than the active voice and also distances you from your writing. Consider, these two ways of saying the same thing:

The man walked the dog. He threw the ball and the dog caught it.

The dog was walked by the man. The ball was thrown by him and it was caught by the dog.

The first statement uses fourteen words and the second twenty, or nearly fifty per cent more. If you are writing a 6,000 word paper then using the passive voice would in theory turn it into a 9,000 word one, with no added value or advantage.

3. Don't completely befuddle and confuse your reader, who may become dispirited and demoralised, by writing in incredibly long, albeit elegant, well constructed and grammatically accurate sentences with numerous sub-phrases, each of them important in its own right, such that the sentence becomes unwieldy, difficult to follow and downright annoying.

4. Develop a good 'ear' for how your writing sounds. We regularly read our own written work aloud to ourselves and others in order to expose our own shortcomings. These include downright howlers, infelicitous expressions, repetitive phraseology, incomplete sentences, fuddled writing, and writing which is too hard to follow or plain ugly. If it can't be read aloud easily and intelligibly then it's not good writing.

5. Develop regular writing habits. It's good to write something, however brief, at least daily.

6. Try to write the way you would speak in order to avoid sounding pretentious. Of course, this won't work if you are uncommonly pretentious in your speech. But remember that the spoken language is often in incomplete sentences and may rely heavily on context and non-verbal communication to convey meaning. Do not write in sentence fragments; rather, compensate with extra clarity and explanation for the lack of non-verbal context.

7. Make effective use of other textual materials beyond the written word such as figures, tables, pictures, photos, diagrams and so on. These can both encapsulate and strengthen the argument being presented.

8. Remember that a sequence in your text does not necessarily constitute an argument. Sometimes we get papers to review which sound a bit like a breathless five-year-old child telling what happened at school that day, 'And then … and then … and then …' This happens when authors are trying to describe what other people

have said or what they have done in their research without any analysis, synthesis or evaluation. You need to construct an argument, not simply give an account.

9. When you are struggling to get your ideas sorted out in your head and don't quite know what it is you want to say, the most useful thing you can do is to talk to some other interested person about them. If no-one is available, Rebecca talks to herself or to the dog. The very process of verbalising your thoughts and arguments helps you to frame and clarify them.

10. Always get other people to read your work before submitting it for possible publication and take their comments seriously.

11. Do not fall into the error of thinking that you can get it right first time and without the help of a significant body of others and several stages of drafting and redrafting.

3   The Business of Publishing

In Chapter 2 we talked about the business of writing and how to go about it. Here we deal with a range of generic issues around the real business of publishing. In Chapters 4 and 5 we will deal with two of the main publishing forms for academics – journal articles and book chapters/ books respectively. In Chapter 6 we talk about some other, slightly more minority sports such as publishing in professional journals.

When to start publishing

The following is adapted from Kenway *et al.*, *Publishing in Refereed Academic Journals: A Pocket Guide* (Deakin University, 1998):

How, when and where to start publishing is not necessarily straight-forward. Some people who are new to publishing feel that they have little to publish unless they have completed a major funded research project or a PhD. Others procrastinate until they feel that they are really on top of all the current literature, and never get beyond the first drafts, frozen in anticipation that the definitive study they need must soon appear. But neither is the case. You are in the position to publish if you:

- Are exploring theories and ideas.
- Have something worthwhile to say on key questions, problems and issues in your field.
- Are seeking to identify some gaps and silences in your area of study and so to contribute to the redefinition of your field.
- Are making conference presentations.

▶

▶
- Are undertaking any research, funded or unfunded.
- Have enrolled on a research degree.
- Are working for someone else's research project as a research assistant or fellow.

Possibly the only reason for hesitating about thinking about publication is if there is a chance that your research may lead to a patent. In some countries, prior publication makes patenting impossible.

What strategies should I have for publishing?

There is no golden rule on what the best publishing strategy is. The most important thing is that you have a strategy and that it fits your needs, work and subject areas. Let's consider, for a moment, three individuals and how they approached the issue.

Nigel is a very laid-back geographer. He works hard at his research and has interesting things to say. However, his publishing trajectory resembles a pleasant and aimless afternoon's stroll more than a purposeful walk from one point to another. He consistently misjudges the contribution he is able to make to his field, undervaluing himself and the appeal of his work. This low self-confidence leads him to wait for publishing opportunities to present themselves rather than going out and proactively seeking them. As a result, his publications are quite randomly distributed across a range of journals which vary in status and prestige. This rather *ad hoc* approach to publishing means that some of Nigel's outputs are in journals that don't have a wide circulation, which are poorly rated in terms of academic status or are in books which disappear quickly without trace. Part of Nigel's dilemma is that he is under considerable pressure to demonstrate 'volume' in his publishing. In a sense, he is being buffeted by the system and his own lack of self-confidence and direction.

Shamila is a young sociologist in a fixed-term, junior lecturing post. She is anxious to gain a tenured permanent position but must demonstrate a good publishing record in order to do so. Shamila is very tempted to publish her work before she really has anything worthwhile to say. Because of the tension between the understandable paucity of her material and the unduly onerous demands on her, she is attempting to 'salami slice' her work (that is, pare very small sections off her research to put in papers in order to generate as many as possible). Because she works in an interdisciplinary way, she is spreading her publications across quite a wide range of journals in different disciplinary fields.

Anthony is a political scientist and a young man in a hurry. He is determined to be recognised as a leader in his field in a short space of time. He has carefully demarcated 'his' research territory and will not stray out of it in undertaking his research. Equally, in publishing, he is highly selective about where he will publish and highly strategic in the placement of his articles and chapters. He has taken careful advice on which are the most prestigious journals in order to achieve maximum recognition by a particular readership. By the same token, Anthony is resistant to any suggestion that he might spread his wings to new fields, and regularly turns down invitations to work and publish with others.

None of these people has got it 100 per cent right or wrong. Your strategy for publishing will be a product of the opportunities that come your way or that you can generate, the nature of your discipline and field, the happenstance of whom you meet and work with and the pressures under which you do your job.

There are a number of important things to bear in mind that arise from Nigel's, Shamila's and Anthony's stories.

- Have confidence about the value of your work and the fact that, if it's good, then someone, somewhere will be interested in reading and publishing it. For instance, an author called Dava Sobel wrote a scholarly book about the development in the eighteenth century of an accurate clock for use at sea to facilitate the determination of the longitudinal position of ships. It doesn't sound like a bestseller, does it? In fact, sales were enormous and the BBC ended up making a widely syndicated drama documentary about it. The lesson is that good work will find an audience, so know the value of what you do.
- It's important to have a sense of where you are going without painting yourself into a publishing corner and declining serendipitous opportunities that might lead to great things. Devise and amend your publishing plan to take good opportunities as they arise.
- What constitutes a good publishing opportunity will invariably change as your career develops. For instance, contributing a chapter to an edited collection is undoubtedly a great opportunity, provided it's a good book, for an early career researcher. It can help you get your name alongside better-established people and help to build your own profile. It also gives you experience of getting published,

and, if the editor is proactive and supportive, this can be a real help in your career generally. Remember, too, that although journals are generally more prestigious, edited books tend to be more widely read. In contradistinction, as your career develops you would probably be best advised to shift the balance of where you publish more heavily towards refereed academic journals and research monographs, choosing contributions to edited collections with care or even becoming the editor of them yourself.

- It's a good idea to publish in a good range of journals, both within and across disciplines, thinking carefully about where you want to be known. Sometimes departments and universities can pressurise academics to publish in particular, highly rated, journals. This is quite short-sighted managerialism. You need to find the best journals for your work. Remember that journals come in and out of favour, especially when it comes to formal research evaluation exercises. Having all your eggs in one basket can therefore be quite a risky strategy as well as one that will minimise the impact that your work makes.

- Try to strike a reasonable balance between the pressures for volume in your publication record as against the importance of achieving quality. Whilst it's good to speak to a number of different audiences, avoid producing a stream of publications, each of which is only marginally different from the one that preceded it. Conversely, it's also good to see a body of published work as something that has intellectual coherence and is reflective of a broader personal intellectual project (as we discuss in *Getting Started on Research*).

Short-termist managerialist pressures to publish or perish in the interests of university finances or narrow careerist considerations, epitomised by the quantity versus quality conundrum, can sometimes blind us to the real importance of publishing. We think it's important to retain the core belief that publishing is about having a sort of written conversation with others in the field. This is its primary purpose, although we are painfully aware of the pressures to publish for publishing's sake that early career academics are all too often subjected to. So, we think that quality should win out, on balance, over quantity. Basically, you have to publish good stuff in reasonable quantities.

Nonetheless some generalisations are possible about this elusive term 'quality'. We think that a good yardstick for quality in academic work is the impact that the publication has in its field. Evaluating impact is a bit like asking how long a piece of string is. Some organisations have attempted to develop pseudo-objective measures of impact, often involving bibliometric methods such as citation analyses. These have been adopted from the natural sciences, where their use is much more prevalent. Bibliometric means what is says: *biblio* = books; *metric* = measurement. A typical method would be to scour academic literature and count the number of times a particular piece is cited. The clear implication is that the more citations there are, the better the piece. It's not rocket science to work out some very fundamental flaws in this approach. First, those who compile citation indices are very selective in the scouring. They choose very specific journals to look for citations in, and these are usually the more mainstream, US-based ones. This can mean that whole areas of work and debate, and even the work of scholars in entire countries, are made invisible by the processes of measurement.

Second, work may be published that other researchers in the field see as tendentious, damaging and/or downright wrong. This can lead to a veritable storm of ripostes and rebuttals, all of which will necessitate citation.

Some people who try to manage the research work of others sometimes latch on to these bibliometric methods in an attempt to divine what the 'best' journals are in order to exhort their long-suffering colleagues to publish in them. For all the reasons we've argued, we feel that such exhortations are wrongheaded. This kind of stuff happens most in the natural sciences but we have all started to see it happen in our own areas. Be on your guard.

Others are not above using bibliometric methods to blow their own publishing trumpet. While this can be a useful device to advance individual careers, we would worry that it lends legitimacy to an illegitimate process and also makes the perpetrator look a bit pathetic. Yet in some Australian universities (and perhaps elsewhere) people are expected to indicate their citation rates in their promotion applications, and there are rumours that they may also be used by key government research-granting bodies as a one means of recognising 'impact'.

So if we can't use bibliometrics, how can we think about impact? This will vary by discipline and field. Here is a range of possible sources of evidence of the impact of your published work.

- Your book is widely (and well) reviewed in journals or one or more of your papers is substantively discussed in a review essay/article in a journal.

- Your work achieves tangible resonance in some way. For instance, it is widely and intelligently discussed and you are frequently cited as a reputable author in certain matters.
- Your work achieves a resonance with policy makers or practitioners. For instance, it may be cited in official reports or there may be some major regulatory/policy change as a result of what you have done. Unfortunately, sometimes governments and others may use your published work without properly acknowledging your intellectual property. The most overt example of this was when, in 2003, it became clear that the British government had plagiarised a (rather elderly) PhD thesis in producing its justification for going to war on Iraq in 2003.
- Your publications spawn further work – what you say and write generates a whole host of work by others that builds upon your starting points.
- You may be identified, through publication, with staking out a whole new field of enquiry.
- You may just get a fantastic response from a variety of different sorts of communities. For instance, you may start attracting research students who want to work with you in your area, get invitations to speak at academic and/or non-academic events or prompt a lot of wider media interest.

Planning your publishing

A good way of ensuring that you have a viable publishing strategy and that you are mindful of the intended impact of your published work, is to have a personal publishing plan. In some institutions you may be required to produce this periodically for the delectation and scrutiny of some manager or mentor. However, the most important reason for having a plan is for your own benefit, and if you do have to produce one for others you will at least be in the fortunate position of not having to do it just for someone else.

A plan, once you have drawn it up, needs to be constantly revisited and updated. It should be a coherent expression of your publishing strategy, aiming to help you achieve the desired impact. A publishing plan is output-oriented, concerned with the tangible products of your work. A bit like the old five-year economic plans of the former USSR, they are usually more honoured in the breach than in the observance and there will be many a slip 'twixt cup and lip. Eisenhower urged his generals to have a cunning plan and execute it ruthlessly, but we don't think you can do that with publishing. So stay flexible and just make sure that the plan becomes something to help guide you in the right direction for you, not a stick to beat yourself with.

Here are some hints on how to plan for publication.

- Set yourself real deadlines for getting stuff done. One of the best ways of doing so is to commit to giving a conference paper – you have to at least do something that won't make you look stupid if you do this. Another good deadline technique is to work with others and mutually commit to deadlines. Most people will let themselves down before other people. If you are not like most people, then this won't work for you, of course.
- If you have something that you think will make a good journal paper, then a classical genealogy for that would be to give the paper at one or more conferences, get feedback and a feel for how/if it works, then write it up for publication.
- Think about the lead times that can be involved in publication. If you want promotion or are subject to a dreaded research review, then don't think that you can start sending things to publishers six months before the crucial date.
- Try to develop a stream of work. Rebecca often gives colleagues the analogy of a production line in a factory – once you have built up a decent pace and are in the rhythm then the whole thing can become self-perpetuating, with the finished goods rolling off the end of the conveyor belt. A steady flow of parallel work will ensure that there are no major peaks and troughs and, if something does go pear-shaped, you know that there is always something else in the pipeline. Don't put all your publication eggs in one basket.
- That said, do bear in mind that people at the start of their career will take some time to build up a steady flow of work. The thought that there is nothing 'in reserve' or 'nearly there' can be quite scary but is common and understandable. All academics, throughout their careers, can experience some peaks and troughs in published and publishable output. You might be working on a major project that involves a lot of fieldwork, or putting all your efforts into one book; or you may experience a personal crisis of some sort. It is not reasonable to expect you to publish at an absolutely steady rate. You

are not a sausage machine, churning out standardised products, and neither should you seek to become one.

- As we said above, avoid always having the same research/writing partners. It's a good idea to plan in a variety of co-authorships and also to do your own stuff independently from time to time.
- Be aware of the expectations within your own discipline for the 'mixture' of published outputs. In some areas research monographs are almost unheard of, whilst in others they are the norm. Some more vocational disciplines expect to see evidence that you have disseminated your research findings to practitioners and policy makers. Whatever the informal rules in your area, work out what they are and try to make sure that you comply.

At this point, you may find it helpful to sit down with your nice hardback research notebook and work out a publishing plan for yourself, or revise one that you already have. You will then be able to read the rest of this book more purposefully.

Authorship

One of the most enduring problems in publishing is the issue of authorship, by which we mean who gets named as an author in the published output and the order of the names on the published piece. If you have done the work all on your own and are the only author, then authorship is not an issue and you can simply put your name alone to the work with a clear conscience. However, many academics both research and write in groups or research teams, and here who gets named as an author can be more problematic.

Authorship conventions differ between disciplines. In the natural sciences co-authorship is the norm, reflecting team research practices. As such, authorship usually includes the whole research team, from principal researchers to technicians and doctoral students. In large multi-sited clinical trials, for example, the list of authors can take up a whole column of text. This is why, in some science, medicine and engineering subjects, senior academics can end up with frighteningly large numbers of publications each year – perhaps as many as fifty or sixty. It doesn't mean that they are working harder than the rest of us, simply that they are collaboratively engaged with a very large team or teams and that, by convention, publications are all authored by the entire team.

Multiple authorship in the arts, humanities and social sciences is now fairly common, or at least not unusual. Unlike the sciences, though, authorship rarely involves more than a small handful of people. Who gets named as an author can be quite tricky and also the result of all kinds of political, careerist and funding pressures. In some countries there may be funding or other imperatives that encourage the exclusion of some people as authors. For instance, there may be research performance evaluation schemes in place that divide the credit by the number of authors or only allow one author to get the credit, or one author in each institution. Sometimes, people who have done quite a lot of work that contributes to a publication may remain completely invisible. We think that this is wrong.

The best way of tackling any problems with attributing authorship is to have clear, early and explicit agreements with your co-authors and fellow researchers. For instance, disbanded project teams may agree among themselves that they can each use the data independently for their own writings, as long as they acknowledge its source.

We think that it is always wisest to err on the side of generosity in such matters. Your colleague may have let you down or annoyed you in some way, but it might have been because of circumstances outside their control and to which you might be subject yourself at a later date. It is *never* worth losing friends in arguments over authorship. In our experience, if you are generous to your colleagues you will rarely be exploited and more likely to get responses such as 'No, I couldn't possibly be named, that wouldn't be fair on you.' At the same time, don't be shy of asserting yourself if you think that someone is deliberately or inadvertently being unfair or attempting to exclude you or minimise your contribution. These can be very hard conversations to have, but you must neither shirk them nor act with bad grace.

There are no hard-and-fast guidelines on who should and shouldn't be named as an author. However, anyone involved in the conception and design of the project, the collection and/or analysis of data, drafting the writing or some critical and substantial revision of it should be seriously considered as an author. One acid test, suggested by Kenway *et al.*, *Publishing in Refereed Academic Journals* (1998), is that if you could present the findings on which the article is based and answer questions about the research theories and design, then you are a potential author – and vice versa.

People should not be considered or cited as authors for academically dishonest reasons – for instance, they are your boss or are being named only to improve publication chances. Similarly, if someone did no real part of the work, or was only marginally involved at the outset of a project, it would be wrong for them to share authorship. With regard to those who act as assistants to projects, the situation can be more fraught and such people can be unfairly treated. We think that if someone did the photocopying, typing or fetched books from the library they don't really have any stake in authorship. Conversely, if they were a valued and hard-working, albeit junior, researcher on the team who did things like the fieldwork or data analysis, then you need to give them the authorship credit they deserve and are likely to need to advance their career.

Megan was a professor responsible for research leadership in a department working hard to improve its research profile. Her junior colleague Isobel asked her to read and comment on a paper that she had written from her PhD. Megan did so and gave quite extensive help. Isobel was grateful for these comments and said to Megan that she wanted to add her name to the list of authors. Megan declined, arguing that, in this instance, she had only done her job and that an acknowledgement for the help would be fine. Megan was additionally concerned that, as the paper was well out of her usual field of work, it would look to the editor that her name had been added to provide additional 'weight' to the authorial line-up. She knew that sharp editors always see through such ruses.

If you are a research assistant employed on someone else's project and you want or need to write on your own for publication utilising the project's work, you must check with the team leader(s) first. They may have other pieces planned in the same area. You may want to write a sole-authored reflective piece about your experiences on the project. If so, it would be a courtesy to let your colleagues know first.

Having established the authors to be named, you need to consider the order in which they will be listed. There are a number of conventions, and our best advice is to choose one, in conjunction with your co-authors, that conforms to expected norms in your discipline and is also appropriate and mutually fair to all. It is important to think hard before departing from normal conventions in your area because doing so can send quite big signals to your readers.

The possible conventions are to:

- *List the authors in descending order of contribution to the research project and/or to the writing of the work.* This method feels like the fairest but can be difficult or impossible to put into practice in such a way that everyone feels they have been fairly dealt with. It can involve comparing apples and pears – what is the relative value of the work of the research assistant in collecting the data as against the principal investigator in conceiving the project initially, when both are essential to the project? Also, it can be just plain hard to work out the relative work input from different people. One author may have done very little, but her input could be the thing that made the whole project work. In a team of peers it might be useful to agree that the person who writes the first draft of a paper becomes the first-named author, for example.
- *List the authors alphabetically by family name.* This is the most straightforward method. By always sticking to alphabetical order, the authorship order does not signal anything significant. We think that, in most circumstances, it is the best method unless you have a co-author called Aaron Aaronovitch who always does very little work.
- *In long-standing writing collaborations, to alternate who goes first in the list of names.* If you have a regular co-author you might consider swapping lead authorship on an alternating basis. If you do this, it's worth letting people know that it is what you have decided to do. Otherwise people will think that there was equal work when the names are alphabetical but that the first named author did more work when they are not.
- *Place a less experienced author first as a means of helping them to build their career.* Well established academics will sometimes do this for their less experienced co-authors. Of course, if you are following the alphabetical convention, they are being generous only if it results in an order that is non-alphabetical. We think that, at times, this can be a right and generous thing to do but that you shouldn't expect people to do it for you as a matter of course. Unfortunately, we see far more instances of people messing around with conventional orderings in order to relegate their more junior co-authors further down the list.

- *Refer to some authors at the end of the list, preceded by the word 'with', as in 'Bloggs, Smith and Jones with Spencer'. Sometimes this use of 'with' which directly signals the far lesser involvement of the final author is wholly appropriate. But don't use it vindictively or in a fit of pique.*

Even if you have acted with care and courtesy in whom you attribute as an author and the order that you place them in, there will still be many people who have helped the publication to happen. These may be colleagues, your own critical friends, conference discussants or reviewers. It is always proper to acknowledge these lesser, albeit vital, inputs in an acknowledgement. However, save the more personal, witty thanks to your cats, the dog and your partner (usually in that order) for books.

A matter of entitlement: titles as totems in academic texts

Basically you need a good title for your work and, sadly, some people can think of them and others can't. If you're in the latter category, get help and advice. Titles fulfil a number of important functions:

- They tell the reader what they are going to read about.
- Most people do their literature search by electronic means, so titles of papers, and especially books, have to contain the types of words that your target readers are likely to type into a search engine.
- The best ones neatly encapsulate and come to symbolise the subject matter of the writing. The very best titles enter into common usage as part of everyday language. An example is Michael Power's *The Audit Society* (1997).
- A good title will entice and titillate the target reader.

You shouldn't be afraid of being creative and imaginative with your titles. But don't go so off the wall so that nobody knows what your piece is about, or you look frivolous, pompous or self-obsessed. Sometimes journal editors or publishers will constrain and shape the titles of your articles, books or chapters. They don't do it out of meanness: they have to consider factors such as the style and feel of the journal, book marketing, page layout (for chapter titles) and house style. While you need to listen to what editors and publishers have to say, you don't have to blindly obey and it's worthwhile entering into a sensible discussion with them if you feel strongly about it.

A final word on the importance of colons. We are traditionalists and believe that the first part of a title should be the snappy, striking, exciting bit: and following the colon should be a subtitle that explains what the thing is really about. However, publishers sometimes prefer it the other way round. This is a matter for negotiation. Alternatively, if you have a *really* good short title, that both tells the reader what the book is about *and* invites them to read on, you can dispense with the colon.

Here are some good and bad examples of titles (you have to decide which is which):

Boyz' Own Stories: Masculinities and Sexualities at School

Pride and Prejudice: Women, Taxation and Citizenship

Was Mickey Mouse a Marxist?

Recipients of Public Sector Annual Reports: Theory and an Empirical Study Compared

Answering Back: Girls, Boys and Feminism in Schools

Failing Boys? Issues in Gender and Education

Teacher Professionalism or Deprofessionalisation? The Consequences of School-based Management on Domestic and International Contexts

Ruling Passions: sexual violence, reputation and the law

Schooling Sexualities

Haunting the Knowledge Economy

Rewards

You are extremely unlikely to gain any significant direct financial return from publishing your research. However, publishing brings its own distinct rewards.

- We can't overemphasise the sheer delight and sense of personal satisfaction that comes from seeing your work in print. Like many pleasures, it is best the first time, but, jaded as we are, we still get a thrill from each new publication.
- Publish or perish. In almost all universities and disciplines, if you do not publish you will not get that new job, promotion, tenure or a much needed pay rise.
- Publishing also helps your university to develop its profile and may bring it financial rewards where there are schemes in place that link funding with the quality and/or volume of staff publications, as in the UK and Australia. This is a case of 'performance pay' – you perform and your university gets paid.
- Publishing brings some closure to the research process. It is part of the dissemination process and there is no point in doing research if you don't tell people about what you have found out.
- It gives you peer standing and esteem in your wider professional community beyond your own university. People you have not met will read your work and know of you and about you (and vice versa). If and when you do eventually meet, you will have a common basis from which to start talking and building networks and friendships.

Of course, some academics do make money out of publishing. However, they either produce textbooks for undergraduates (where the market can be very large) or they write for the popular media. There are some, but not many, research-based books which become popular on student reading lists or which get picked up and made the core reader for some big undergraduate courses even though they are not textbooks. These can make quite a bit of money – but not nearly enough to live on. A few academics write popular novels (usually about universities). It is possible that they make money – certainly they must make more out of such work than out of their research publications.

IPR (otherwise known as Intellectual Property Rights)

This stuff can seem quite scary because it's all to do with the law. However, it's important to understand the basics about IPR, both to protect your own interests and to ensure that you don't fall foul of the law.

Because creativity, knowledge and innovation can lead to the financial and other rewards that we outlined above, people have found it desirable to develop ways in which individuals and organisations can establish their ownership of such 'assets'. This is called intellectual property (IP). 'Intellectual Property Rights' (IPR) is the term used to refer to the system of law designed to facilitate the protection and exploitation of IP by its owners. Legal arrangements differ from country to country, often quite markedly.

There are four main types of IPR: patents (for inventions); trade marks (for brand identity); designs (for product appearance); and copyright (for material such as literary and artistic outputs, music, films, sound recordings, broadcasts, software and multimedia). Here we are concerned only with copyright issues.

Generally, copyright does not have to be registered with any government agency. This is the big difference between copyright and patents for inventions. Copyright protection is therefore automatic for the creator. Copyright is time-limited. The exact amount of time varies from country to country and according to the type of material but is usually upwards of twenty-five years.

Copyright gives the creator of a written text (as well as any other material created, such as videos or multimedia artefacts) the *moral right* to be identified as the creator of the material. This is your legal protection against plagiarists or those who seek to remove your name from co-authored work – although recourse to law usually won't get you anywhere unless you can prove substantive loss as a result of your right being breached. Your moral right also allows you to object to the distortion or mutilation of your creative work.

Copyright also gives the *economic right* to control the use of the work in a number of ways. This includes making copies, publishing copies, performing in public, broadcasting and use on-line. What usually happens when your work is accepted for publication is that you have to assign your economic copyright to the publisher. This enables the publisher to economically exploit your work, allowing them to cover their costs and also to (hopefully) make a profit. In return for this assignment of rights, the publisher may agree to make some payment to you. The form of payment varies with the format of the material. We've set out the usual way in which it works below.

- *Journal articles.* No money payment is made to the author(s). However, the publisher usually gives the author(s) a free copy of the journal in which the article appears and/or a number of offprints. Some publishers support their journals by giving the editors money for secretarial assistance. However, and increasingly, journals are so short of funds that they sometimes charge authors a submission fee on papers, or even a publication fee. This is particularly the case with small journals in low to middle-income countries and indeed some US journals, where the publishers make a big fat profit but still charge the authors.
- *Book chapters.* Usually a (very) small lump sum is offered to the author(s) and they get a copy of the book in which it appeared. Sometimes the lump sum can be taken in the form of books from the publisher's list to a slightly greater value than the cash. When you agree to write a chapter for an edited collection it is worth checking with the editors to see how they plan to distribute the money. In such circumstances you need to think about how well the book may sell – if it is to be a student textbook you might ask for a share of the royalties.
- *Authored and edited books.* The author(s)/editors usually get a royalty payment based on a percentage of the net receipts (sales less direct costs) that the publisher derives from the sales of the book or the sales of the rights to publish it in, for example, another language or geographical area. Some publishers will offer an advance on royalties and when you edit a book the payments to contributors are made out of such advances (i.e. it is you who pays them, not the publisher). You will usually also get a few free copies of the book.

Most academics are employed by a university. Because academics are employees, under some legal systems, the products of their work may strictly belong to their employer. Universities worldwide are ever anxious to maximise their income and IP can represent just such an additional source of income. However, they are usually most interested in patents, where the profits to be had are at least potentially significant. As we've already demonstrated, the money at stake from copyright in academic outputs is usually small fry in comparison. As a result, most universities allow most staff to reserve to themselves the copyright in their work and any resulting income. However, you should check out your own university's position on this. Sometimes, when people are working in research units within institutions, especially self-financing ones, staff give permission or are required to assign the economic copyright in their work to the institution or the research unit.

It is important to understand that, when you assign your economic copyright to a publisher, it is no longer yours. This is a legal undertaking and you must take it seriously. For instance, if you are asked for permission to reprint something you have written (for instance, to reproduce a journal article in a student reader), the permission is not yours to give. You must ask your publisher and they may or may not give it. In the past, publishers were always willing to give such permission for journal articles, as long as the original source was acknowledged. However, we know of instances where such permission has been refused because the publisher wants to sell papers from back copies of journals over the Internet ('Click here, pay $15 and download'). Publishers may be less obliging with regard to books, as they have a longer shelf life. If publishers do consent, they may charge the other publisher. If they do sell the rights to your work in this or any other way, you will get some kind of payment as agreed in your original contract.

Of course, all this stuff to do with copyright applies to other people's work as much as to your own. This means that if you want to use excerpts, diagrams, photographs and so on from someone else's published work, you must respect their economic copyright and moral right of attribution. With regard to economic copyright, there are always circumstances in which you can reproduce limited amounts of someone else's work, for the purposes of critique, commentary and research. You must make yourself familiar with the rules in your own particular country.

Authors' societies

There are a number of authors' societies around the world that help authors get the benefit of payments made for the photocopying or lending of their work. There is usually a small fee payable for joining it, but this is usually more than offset by the income stream which members receive. For instance, in Australia you can claim money for lending rights from the Educational Lending Rights Scheme and for copying from the Copyright Agency. In the UK there is a body called the Authors' Licensing and Collecting Society.

Publishing Articles in Academic Journals

Having covered the basics, we turn our attention in this chapter to some of the complexities and details of how to write journal articles and get them published in refereed academic journals.

What do we mean, 'academic journals'?

We find that undergraduate students often get confused about the difference between academic literature and other sorts of publication when doing literature reviews. This is often because we haven't been specific enough about what we mean by 'academic journals'. What we do mean are publications, on paper or electronic, which contain scholarly articles that present some or all of the following: research findings, new knowledge, new theorisations or interesting syntheses or re-presentations of existing knowledge. The authors and the readers are usually academics, but not necessarily so.

Academic journals are, therefore, the 'chat rooms' for the exchange of knowledge and ideas and for debate. In fact, this is exactly the reason why the scientific community invented academic journals in the eighteenth century. They were, and remain, an important mechanism by which geographically disparate scholars can communicate and share their thinking.

Journals have a particular structure. They are always edited by one or more academics, who take overall responsibility for the shape and character of the journal. They generally also have editorial boards, usually drawn from the international academic community and chosen to reflect the range of interests of the journal. They may be more or less actively engaged in the processes of publishing the journal. Journals come out regularly, usually three or four times a year, and from time to time may have special issues edited by guest editors on particular themes. In most cases, however, each edition of the journal will present a fairly eclectic mix of papers, but all within the broad remit of the particular journal.

Another common misconception, but this time more often among postgraduate students and less experienced faculty, is that articles in professional journals are on a par, in research terms, with refereed papers in academic journals. Be in no doubt about this, among academics, academic journals are much more prestigious. But of course, writing for appropriate professional audiences is a means of achieving good dissemination of your work to those who might use it in theirs is important.

Some people think that writing for professional audiences is a good apprenticeship for doing academic writing. Indeed, early publication in professional journals can boost people's confidence, stimulate access to research fields and also help people experience the personal satisfaction of getting into print. But, these benefits are sometimes all too elusive and outweighed by two very serious risks.

First, the two genres are quite distinct, albeit related, forms. Professional journal articles based on academic research are really translations of academic writing for lay readerships. That is, they represent an attempt to render academic work more accessible to a wider audience. Logically, therefore, it is not possible to write for professional audiences before the academic thinking and writing have been done. Further, given that the genres are quite different, the writing skills you need to write for one do not necessarily translate into writing for the other.

Second, some inexperienced academics spend so much time and effort on writing for practitioners that they never engage with academic audiences, convincing themselves that they have done the academic job when really they haven't. A further problem for such people is that the quality of their writing for professionals is frequently rather poor because it is not grounded in the rigorous thinking and peer review processes that academic journals demand and provide. In short, putting the professional before the academic means that this stuff simply doesn't go through the academic mill and is therefore unrefined and unimproved.

Jennifer had established herself as a successful writer for the technical, professional press prior to commencing her research career. For these audiences, and for editors who paid by word length, she had developed a style that was very terse and directly factual. When she started her PhD, it took a long time for her to adapt her writing style to the more discursive, carefully argued approaches that are needed in academic writing.

Why publish in academic journals?

As an academic, you will probably have been subject to quite strong pressure from your institution to publish in academic journals, often because more publications mean more external funding for the university. Pressure to publish may also come from competition for internal promotion. However much universities say officially that they promote people for their teaching excellence, this is often patently untrue. Teaching is virtually always a secondary consideration when committees think about whether someone should be promoted or not. Whilst these pressures to publish are very real and often quite painful, we believe that you should not lose sight of the many much more positive reasons for doing such work.

- Publishing is academic journals is usually an immensely personally rewarding activity that can offer you a sense of progress, 'closure' as you finish one phase of your research, achievement and pride in yourself and your work.
- If you don't publish your work in academic forums you are failing to engage in wider academic debates or add to the body of publicly available knowledge in your field – which is one of the primary purposes of undertaking research in the first place. Remember that reading other people's refereed work helps academics to develop their own thinking, research and teaching.
- The rigorous review processes that your work will undergo will give it a certain standing or 'quality mark'. It is rare for papers to emerge from the review process unimproved – even if bruised authors are sometimes reluctant to admit it. Readers are likely to trust something that is as well written as it can be and which they know has been subject to scrutiny.

This is especially the case if you are trying to influence non-academic readers who might use or engage with your research.

- Quite simply, publishing helps you to build your reputation and that of your research and field. This may be crucial to getting new jobs or promotion.
- If you make a contribution to the research income of your department and/or university by achieving a good publication record, you will indirectly benefit by being a member of a more conducive and better-funded research environment.
- A good publication record will also help when it comes to winning external research funding by making you look more credible. We deal with this subject in *Winning and Managing Research Funding*.

What can I publish?

The first key consideration in deciding whether to publish or not is whether you have anything worthwhile to say at this point. Premature publication is frustrating, messy and really to be avoided. Therefore do not waste your energies and efforts and those of journal editors and peer reviewers or try the patience of readers. Conversely, don't be so coy about your writing that you constantly delay submitting anything for publication because it isn't yet 'perfect'. Perfection is a chimera – it can't be achieved and you can waste a lot of time and energy seeking the holy grail of the Perfect Publishable Paper.

Here is a list of the sorts of papers that you might be interested in writing for publication:

- A paper describing and analysing your empirical or archival data from a research project. This can be written at various stages in the research process – you don't have to wait until the project is completed to write about it. Often researchers find it useful to publish 'along the way' once they have appropriate data to comment on. Of course, you should publish articles (and/or books) on completed research projects too.
- Most journals have special issues around particular themes from time to time. The themes are generally broad and, with imagination, you may be able to craft your research into a paper that fits them.

- A review essay, which takes a critical look at a range of literature in your field, synthesising it and building on it to develop new insights. This can be a good one if you are doing a doctorate and therefore having to really master a whole field of literature.
- A 'think piece' which develops theoretical insights and ideas within your field of enquiry.
- A response to someone else's work. You are more likely to do this when you disagree with someone, but sometimes journals invite specific individuals to respond to a particular piece of work.
- A methodological reflection in which you explore problems and dilemmas that may have arisen in the course of your research. Some fields give rise to much more of this kind of writing than others.
- Some journals have slots for shorter, less developed 'work in progress' reports. These may include a fairly straightforward description of an on-going research project. They can be a good way of getting into print when you are relatively inexperienced or anxious to get a major project 'on the map'.
- Other journals invite 'opinion pieces' about issues that are of current importance. These, too, tend to be shorter than the journal's regular articles and may be more polemic in style.
- Some canny people planning their doctoral theses do so in such a way that they can develop papers for publication in parallel with their dissertation chapters. In this way, they give themselves confidence that their work passes muster; polish, through the refereeing process; and a significant career advantage when they start applying for jobs.

Keep in mind, though, that some of the sorts of pieces listed above may not be peer-reviewed. Whilst you will need to make clear the level of scrutiny to which your paper was subjected, even non-refereed pieces can help to build careers and reputations, especially in the early stages.

What makes a publishable paper?

Even though the types of refereed papers that you might publish can vary enormously, there are generic qualities that journal editors and referees look for in all of them. Good publishable papers will have a majority, if not all, of the following characteristics. This list is adapted from Kenway *et al.*, *Publishing in Refereed Academic Journals* (1998):

- They present new knowledge, either in the form of substantive research findings, theoretical developments, new insights into existing debates, new analyses of existing knowledge or a synthesis of the literature.
- They are grounded in the relevant literature, demonstrating familiarity and engagement in an on-going academic conversation.
- They address new or familiar issues pertinent to the discipline or field.
- They ask and attempt to answer provocative questions in a persuasive manner.
- They are well written, with carefully crafted and sustained arguments.

How do I get my paper published?

Taking a paper from the first twinkle in your eye through to publication is, unfortunately, quite a long and complicated process. Below we take you through the seven stages from start to finish. Figure 1 presents these stages in diagrammatic form.

Stage one: getting ideas, doing research and writing

If you haven't even started on this stage, you need to read *Getting Started on Research* and also Chapter 2 of this book.

Stage two: giving conference and seminar papers

Once you have developed a paper you really need to take it on the road – taking it to conferences, seminars and workshops. Within reason, a good paper can't have too many outings – but watch that you don't give the same paper to the same people again and again. We deal with conference papers in detail in *Building Networks*.

It's important to use conferences, seminars and workshops as a way of getting feedback so that you can reflect on, refine and polish your paper until you have buffed it up enough to be sent to a journal. You can

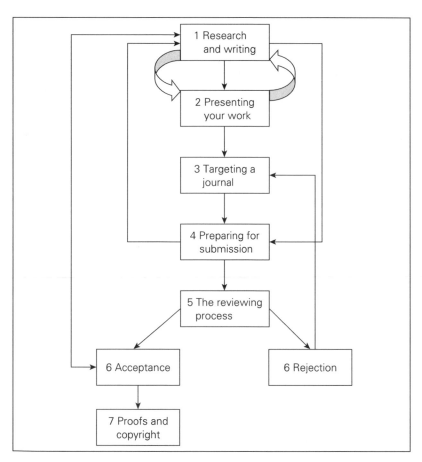

FIGURE 1 Seven steps to heaven: Stages in getting a paper published

be sure that if you keep getting similar adverse comments when you present the paper, your reviewers will also discern the weaknesses when you submit it unless you have resolved the problems. It may be a matter of explaining more carefully what you mean or addressing more fundamental issues. On the other hand, if your paper stimulates lively discussion and interest, it signals that you have struck a rich seam from which to publish. Be careful to take good notes on what people say about your work. Write these up either during your session or immediately afterwards. If you feel that you can't cope with presenting your paper, answering questions on it and taking notes of people's comments and suggestions, get a friend or colleague in the audience to do the note taking for you.

Stage three: targeting a journal

Okay, you have written a paper that has been well aired, commented upon and subsequently and iteratively improved. Now you need to identify an appropriate journal to eventually send it to.

Finding the right journal takes time and effort. But investment at this stage will save you much energy and grief later on. Not all journals, as you will be aware, are the same. They embody different areas of interest, styles, methodologies, aims and objectives. You must achieve a reasonable degree of congruence between your paper and the target journal. Inevitably this involves some compromise in both how you rewrite the paper and the journals you try to get published in.

You will already have some idea about journals from your own research and reading for it. However, here are some more suggestions about how to initially locate journals that may be interested in your work.

- You could do a lot worse than consider the journals that you have been reading for your research. If you find what they publish interesting and relevant, it is likely that your work will fit well.
- Go to the library and browse through the journals on the shelves. All of them will have notes for contributors and statements of editorial policy, usually inside the front or back cover. You should also scan the articles in their back issues to get a sense of whether your work is congruent with the journal's remit and style. This can be a good way of shaping your thinking about where work might be placed. Be imaginative and a bit eclectic about what you look at and don't necessarily confine yourself to a narrow sphere of interest.
- Go to the websites of the substantial publishers of journals and look through their lists of journals. Various search engines, especially in library databases of journals, will take you to these sites. There you will be able to search for journals in particular disciplinary or interest areas. Each journal will have its own page, including its editorial policy, sample issues and articles (for free download) and notes for contributors.
- Ask your mentors or more experienced colleagues for suggestions. But beware – the increasing preponderance of research quality measurement exercises has often tended to lead to a mindless, lemming-like rush for certain journals that achieve iconic status. If your work fits nicely with such journals, all well and good.

However, we would strongly counsel against twisting and distorting your papers in order to try to squash them into a particular journal box they do not fit.

- Sign up for the various journal electronic alert lists that are available. These can take the form of simply giving you the contents pages of journals in your sphere of interest, or may give you abstracts of articles. You can put in your own key words and, provided you choose them sensibly, this will be a useful way of finding out which journals publish your kind of stuff.

Handy hints for targeting journals

We have told you how to look for journals, but what exactly are you looking for? Remember that you need to take a really focused, strategic approach to this important task.

1. The stated editorial policy and your impression of the papers carried should give you a clear picture of the kinds of themes and issues that the journal seeks to address. Eliminate those journals that really have no interest in your areas of concern, broadly construed.

2. Sometimes journals have a particular epistemological, theoretical or indeed political leaning, either stated or unstated. By and large, you should respect these stances and not send your work to a journal that is patently out of sympathy with your own stances. On the other hand, sometimes you may be pleasantly surprised to find that journals with a reputation for publishing only papers of a certain type would actually welcome a broader range of submissions. This is most likely to be the case where the editorial approach is non-positivist because, by its nature, such thinking is open to differing notions of knowledge creation (see also *Getting Started on Research*). If in doubt, it's always worthwhile contacting the editors and sending them a short abstract of your article to check out whether it is the kind of thing that, in principle, they would consider.

3. Journals have different attitudes to publishing a range of styles of writing. Some will welcome experimental writing or poetry. Others are committed to the standard academic generic forms. If you

have written something experimental or unconventional, there is little point in sending it to a journal that does not and will not include that kind of writing.

4. Look at the list of editors and the editorial board to see whether the people included do your kind of work or are interested in it. Some journals also publish an annual list of people not on the editorial board who have reviewed papers for them. It's worth looking at this to see what kinds of people are receiving the papers. Don't send a paper to a journal that regularly uses reviewers who might be unsympathetic to your work and/or your area.

5. There are a number of practical issues to which you must also pay attention. For instance, journals accept articles of different lengths. Some want very short submissions while others are prepared to accept much longer articles. This will be stated in the guidelines for authors inside the back or front cover of the journal and on their web page. Failure to heed these guidelines makes editors very grumpy.

6. Journals have different turn-round times for the refereeing process and lead times for publication when accepted. Sometimes this information appears in the journal itself as a footnote to each paper. There are a number of complex factors that impact on lead times. The vagaries of research quality assessment exercises can mean that there is a rush to publish before the exercise deadlines, swamping journals. Sometimes editors seek to cluster papers that they think fit well together. Putting an edition of a journal together can be a complex jigsaw puzzle, especially as editors are limited in the number of pages they are allowed to have in each issue. This means that you may be moved up or down the queue, depending on the length of your paper, as they try to make the most economical use of the space available. If getting your work out within a tight period is crucial to you, then you should check out all these issues with the editor before you submit. New journals can be a good place to send your articles if you want them out quickly, as they are often in search of good material in order to make an impact with their early issues.

7. You should keep an eye open for information about upcoming special issues that may suit your work. These will be put together within a particular time frame and the guest editors often need to solicit, review and accept the appropriate number of articles quite quickly.

8. Pay attention to whom the journal is aimed at. It is, for example, a waste of time to send an article that has relevance only within your own national boundaries to a journal that promotes itself as being about genuinely international issues.

9. An increasing number of journals charge authors for submission or publication of papers. These charges can be substantial. If your institution does not pick up such fees, or you have to negotiate it, then that is another consideration in your journal selection. It is also a consideration to be built into any research funding applications.

10. Conversely, in the UK at least, funds exist to encourage journals to publish papers from academics in low to middle-income countries. Moreover, journals gain international prestige by showing that they attract authors from a wide range of countries. What can sometimes look like a closed shop isn't necessarily so.

11. Don't waste your time and energies trying to get published in a journal if you have had a huge argument with the editor. Conversely, try not to fall out with important journal editors.

12. Try to pick journals that you wish your name and work to be associated with – generally those that will help you to gain prestige and academic standing in a particular area. Thus journal selection becomes an important part of your networking and career-building work.

13. As time goes on and you build up your publications record, spread your wings a bit and don't always publish in the same place or places. At the same time, it is good to develop a relationship with the editors of particular journals, and you may want to publish in some places more than others. The key here is to keep the right balance.

14. Get to know editors by getting yourself introduced to them or going to their presentations at conferences. You can help to build up a good relationship with journals by undertaking what are sometimes regarded as thankless tasks, such as doing book reviews. As time goes on, and you get more established, you may be asked to be a reviewer or referee for articles submitted to the journal. It's always a good idea to be helpful and amenable in doing such work because then you will be regarded as a good friend of the journal. It won't mean that bad papers get published or that you will have an easier ride, but it may help to ensure that you and your papers are dealt with promptly and efficiently.

Again, this is part of building a network within your academic community (see *Building Networks* for more on this). Having such a relationship will help you to approach the editor with your ideas and have constructive discussions about how to take them forward.

15. The single most important thing in choosing where to publish is to select journals which suit your work, which you are interested in and which allow you to make the best possible impact. Other things being equal, however, try to target the most prestigious journal that you realistically have a chance of getting your work into.

Journals are often ascribed 'national' or 'international' labels. As a matter of course, virtually all journals seek to be seen as international. If we started picking at the thread of what makes a journal national or international, we could fill the rest of this book. Ultimately, whether a journal is of national or international importance is a matter of judgement. The international relevance of research, even if it deals with a local subject, is a key marker of excellence. For journals, an international dimension is a necessary but not sufficient condition for excellence. That international dimension might be connoted by the breadth of the editorial board and the origins of the articles but, most important, by whether the papers themselves are capable of speaking to audiences beyond narrow national boundaries.

Stage four: preparing your paper for submission

The task of preparing your paper for submission to a journal is quite complex; Figure 2 shows the process. Preparing a paper for submission involves the synthesis of three important constituent elements: your pre-existing paper, the feedback that you will have received on it and the specific requirements and characteristics of your target journal. We call this process 'drafting and crafting'. What you will be doing is gently moulding your paper so that it is beautifully written, academically robust and irresistible to your target journal. When you have done this, you will need one last round of polishing before your 'baby' is ready to go off.

For this stage you should already have the draft paper, feedback and journal requirements to hand. You can't start without them. There are two key aspects to drafting and crafting: content and form. Both need

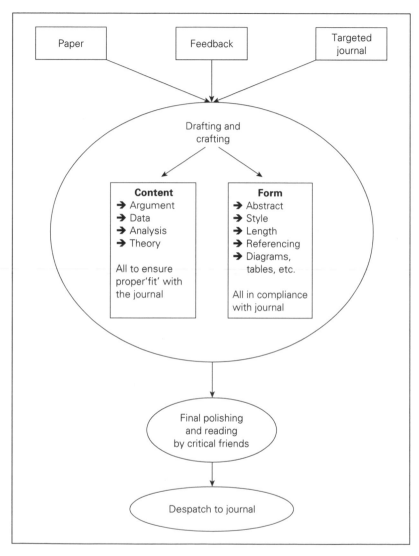

FIGURE 2 Preparing a paper for submission to a journal

to be carefully addressed if you are to be successful in getting your work published. The two textboxes below give you a checklist of things that you have to pay close attention to. You may also find it helpful to refer to *Getting Started on Research* and Chapter 2 of this book.

Content

- Has your paper got a carefully sequenced, logically organised argument that fits together and works like the finest Swiss clock-work? If so, is it explicit, so that you minimise the amount of work the reader has to do?
- Is there a clear and strong relationship between the argument and any evidence, data or other material that you have used?
- Is your analysis of any evidence, data or other material method-ologically sound, clearly described and well justified?
- Have you drawn on appropriate theoretical resources and used them in ways that elucidate your arguments rather than obscure them? Are you sure that you have properly understood the theory that you have used? Do not, on any account, rely on deriva-tive writings, as interpretations by others may be misleading or inappropriate.
- Overall, does your paper 'sit' well with the kind of work published in the journal and your intended audience?
- Finally, and most important, is your work credible as a publishable paper, albeit possibly with some revision? You must on no account use the journal review process instead of doing the drafting and crafting work yourself with the assistance of critical friends/mentors/advisers/supervisors and taking the paper around to conferences and seminars.

Form

- The overwhelming majority of journals require an abstract along with the paper. This is a very short (usually 150–200 words) summary of what the paper says. Abstracts are important because, if or when your paper is published, the abstract will be used by potential readers in deciding whether your work may be of value to them. Reviewers of your paper may also utilise the abstract as part of their work. Brevity does not mean that this is an easy thing to get right. Make sure that the abstract matches what the paper is actually about.

▶
- Have you written your paper in the designated house style of the journal? For example, have you complied with guidelines on matters such as capitalisation, the spelling conventions, the use and positioning of footnotes and/or endnotes, punctuation and so on?
- It is vital that you adhere rigorously to the designated referencing style of the journal, so that all your references are complete, none has been omitted and there are no redundant ones from earlier drafts. This will be easy if you have taken our advice in *Getting Started on Research* and invested in a good bibliographic database package. Otherwise, you will just have to be pedantically methodical and careful. Failure to adhere to referencing guidelines is a major source of aggravation for editors and a good way to get on their bad sides. Consider it to be one of the Seven Deadly Sins.
- Is the layout of your paper on the page clear and comprehensible? Does it follow the guidelines for the journal? For instance, most journals ask you to include diagrams, graphs, pictures and so on as appendices with a note in the text where the typesetters should insert them. Usually journals request that the manuscript is double-spaced and that your name does not appear anywhere other than on the title page (except possibly in the bibliography, although you may choose to insert 'author' here instead of your name). We explain below why this is an important requirement.
- Is your paper a suitable length for the journal? Sometimes this is expressed as the number of words (usually by non-US journals), whilst US journals commonly use a page (i.e. 'letter size') length. Watch out for the fact that US paper sizes can vary quite markedly from those used elsewhere.
- Are your diagrams, graphs, figures, tables, pictures and so on clearly labelled, of good quality and obviously related to the written text? Don't rely on colour unless you know that the journal will use colour printing.
- Don't ferget to use the spillchicker. Don't rely on it entirely, as some misspellings don't get picked up. Rebecca once missed a critical 'l' off her curriculum vitae when talking about her 'public sector research'. Grammar checkers is sometimes helpful too, but didn't rely on it because their often wrong.

Your paper is almost ready to go. Whilst we caution against obsessive polishing which actually rubs the gilt off, it is worth while at this stage to get your critical friends and mentors to give the thing a final read over if they have the time and interest. Whilst you should be your own best critic by this stage, they may pick up on things that you, because of your closeness to the work, have missed. If time permits, put your paper away for a few days and then come back to it with fresh eyes and re-read it. A little bit of distance can really help you to see the wood for the trees. At this point you may do a bit of final tweaking, but it shouldn't be much. This may all sound like hard work, and it is. But you should be proud of your work and want it to be seen in the best possible light.

Finally, at last, you are ready to despatch it. All journals make it a condition of submission that the article is being sent only to them. Abide by this rule or you will lose credibility with editors and peer reviewers. There is a sensible reason for it – the reviewing process is time-consuming and expensive hard work for all involved. Nobody wants to go though it, thinking they are helping you, when you are in fact two-timing them.

You now have to write a letter to the editor. We think that it is a good idea to introduce yourself if you are likely to be unknown to them. If you do know them (perhaps because you have been doing good networking work at conferences, etc.) then remind them where they met you and perhaps what they said. If they know your doctoral supervisor/adviser or mentor, then remind them of that too. Don't be pushy, but do exude a nice quiet confidence that you are a worthy author moving in the right circles and doing interesting things. Tell them a little bit about what the paper is about (maybe just one sentence), but don't repeat the abstract. It can also be helpful to explain a bit of the paper's background – perhaps that it is derived from work on a major funded project or how you came to be doing it. Keep all this networking and contextual information very brief.

Check the journal's requirements regarding submission – do they want hard copies (if so, how many) and a computer disk or are they willing to accept electronic copies only? If so, will they accept them by email or do they want a disk? Keep your own copies of what has been despatched. Make a note of the date, but do bear in mind that the next stage (see below) can take a very long time, so you need to put it towards the back of your mind and not worry. Finally, put it all in the post/send the email and go out and celebrate in whatever way floats your boat.

Stage five: the waiting game – the review process

We thought you might find it useful to have a description of what happens to your paper while you are doing all that waiting.

When the journal editor receives your paper the first thing that they will do is to give it a quick read-over to check the following things:

- That the paper is in the right area for the journal and that, for example, you are not a dentist who has accidentally sent a paper to the *International Journal of Oral History*.
- It is in the required format for the journal or near enough so that it is worth sending out for review.
- Whether it is intended for a special issue or the regular journal, and any other exceptional issues that you may have raised in your covering letter.
- Most important, they will check whether it is of a sufficiently high standard to be worth sending out to review. Editors are very aware of how hard academics work and of what a lot of work it is to review a paper properly. They don't want to alienate their all-important pool of reviewers by sending out papers that wouldn't pass an undergraduate examination.

Gender and Education is the leading feminist journal in education. As such, it is committed to assisting inexperienced and/or unsupported academics to be able to publish in it. The journal rule is that all articles must be reviewed by at least one member of the 20-member editorial board. It became apparent that the review process of the journal was being used by authors as a kind of work avoidance, with too many half-baked papers being sent in and reviewed time and time again. This placed an intolerable burden on the editorial board and, indeed, on other reviewers. As a result, the board decided that papers could no longer be resubmitted more than once.

A good editor who is unhappy with your paper at this stage will send it back to you with a letter of explanation. Once the editor is satisfied, they will do two things. First, they will send you an acknowledgement informing you that they have received your paper and sent it out for review. If you have sent a paper off and don't hear anything for a month, it is worthwhile emailing the editor politely to double-check that the paper has actually been received. However, you should not hassle and harry. Second, they (or their administrative assistant) will remove the title page with your name on it from the manuscript. They will also check to make sure that your name doesn't appear in other places, such as the headers or footers, and that you have not cited yourself in ways that identify you as the author. If you are identifiable in any way, they may well ask you to resubmit the paper rather than compromise the blind peer review process.

The editor will then give it a reference number and send it to at least two selected referees together with the journal's evaluation sheet, which asks them to comment on various aspects of your paper and to indicate whether it is publishable. Part of their response will be intended for your eyes but the editor may also offer them the opportunity to make comments just for the editor's eyes.

Who are these referees? They will usually be experienced academics and researchers whose expertise fits them well to critically evaluate the suitability of your paper for publication. Although they will not officially know who the author of a paper is, they may well be able to guess if they have been busy out and about at conferences or reading the journals in which you have previously published. They will usually not be people in your own institution or whose help you acknowledge, although this has been known to occur.

The reviewers will be asked to return the paper within a limited period – often about six weeks. However, because this is the kind of work that academics struggle to find space to do, papers for review often get relegated to the bottom of the pile and they do not manage to meet their deadlines. What this means is that the poor old editor (or their administrative assistant) will have to write reminding them that they have a paper to review. How quickly such a reminder is sent out after the due date for the review depends very much on the journal's administrative resources. You can help yourself here by submitting the best possible paper that precisely meets the journal's requirements. A well written paper on an interesting topic will incite the reviewer to do their work much more promptly than one that they approach with dread terror. This is another reason to write a really sparkly abstract, as nine of out ten reviewers will at least scan it when they open the envelope/attachment from the editor before putting the article at the bottom of their overflowing in-tray.

It has to be said that reviewers vary in quality. Some do a wonderful job whilst others are vindictive, destructive and self-obsessed or just plain lazy. They are so heterogeneous that we can't begin to describe the gamut of behaviours. However, we give you below two completely fictional pen portraits of the Reviewer from Hell and the Reviewer as Angel.

The Reviewer from Hell

Professor Nick Beelzebub is not really an active researcher and is living on his past reputation. However, he always agrees to undertake reviews because he enjoys the power it gives him as a gatekeeper over his younger and evidently brighter peers. He delights in tearing a paper to pieces without making any constructive suggestions for revision. He is firmly fixed in his own research paradigm and will not countenance any alternatives. His comments on others' papers always start from the premise that they should have adopted his favoured approach and the fact that they haven't means that the research is valueless. That is, he never judges anybody's work on its own merits but only by reference to his own beliefs. The reviews are peppered with unfortunate and hurtful phraseology such as 'the author completely fails ...', 'this is weak and insubstantial work' and so on. Old Nick has no regard for the feelings of the nervous authors who will be receiving his commentaries. It is either impossible to divine from his reviews what needs to be done to make the paper publishable or his demands are completely unrealistic and inappropriate.

The Reviewer as Angel

Professor Angelica Hope is a successful academic, who is quietly confident about her own abilities and expertise. She undertakes reviewing work assiduously although she has trouble fitting it in with her heavy work load. This means that she sometimes keeps papers for longer than she would really wish to. Her comments are invariably honest, straightforward and constructive. She aims to help authors

▶ present their own work and ideas in the best way for them and the journal. When asking for a paper to be revised, she will give very clear and precise advice on how to go about it. She may recommend additional literature that would be useful or further analysis work. When she has finished writing her comments, she carefully rereads them and tries to imagine herself as the author receiving them, asking herself the question 'How would I feel if these comments were about my work?' This doesn't mean that she never has negative things to say. Furthermore, if she really thinks that a paper is unsalvageable, she will say so and explain why.

Once the editor has, eventually, received the reviewers' comments they can make a judgement about what should happen to your paper. The editor's job is a crucial one at this stage, as they may have to arbitrate between reviewers who disagree or make judgement calls about how much they should encourage you to revise the paper and resubmit it to them. Whatever the decision, the editor will write to you explaining it and enclosing any reviewers' comments. Opening that envelope/email can stimulate emotions from ecstasy to despair and dread terror and/or extreme anger. These emotional reactions are never completely attenuated, no matter how senior people become. You need to allow yourself to have the reaction but then think about how to move your paper along. A number of different sorts of editor's decisions are possible.

Scenario 1, and very unlikely, your paper may be accepted as it stands with no revisions or amendments. Let's be frank, this is very unusual so don't beat yourself up if it doesn't happen to you.

Scenario 2, the editor may accept the paper subject to relatively minor amendments that do not require it to be sent out for review again. The sorts of things you might be asked to do are, for example, to clarify the use of diagrams or graphs, to define your terms better, to strengthen the introduction or conclusion, to rewrite the abstract more clearly or to improve the referencing. This is far from an exhaustive list – it's just meant to give you a feel for the kinds of things regarded as minor revisions.

Scenario 3, and a very common category, you may be asked to make major revisions and then resubmit for reconsideration by reviewers.

Here the kinds of revision required will be more substantive and may require quite significant reworking either of the theory or data analysis or the structure of the paper. Reviewers should give you quite detailed and clear feedback on exactly what needs to be done and you need to pay careful attention to it.

Scenario 4, your paper may be rejected outright. Rather like asking someone you really fancy out on a date, rejection invariably hurts. There are many types of rejection and many reasons why a paper may be rejected. For instance, the paper may be deemed inappropriate for the journal. If that happens, you should not have had to wait too long, as a good editor should have picked this up before sending it out for review. In such a circumstance, some editors will offer suggestions of alternative journals to which you might submit the paper. Alternatively, the paper may be deemed irredeemably poor and not capable of sufficient improvement to make it publishable in that particular journal. Remember that no judgement is truly objective and that the reviewers' and editors' decisions may be prompted by fundamental epistemological or theoretical differences – they may simply not see the world in the same way that you do. Alternatively, the quality of your work may not have been very good and the reviewers should explain clearly in what ways your paper is deficient.

> Barry received a hurtful rejection on a piece of important work that he had been doing. He realised that he had sent it to the wrong journal when one reviewer wrote, 'Why does the author keep saying things like "Our interviews showed" – qualitative interviews can show "nothing".' Barry subsequently revised the paper slightly and it appeared in a prestigious edited collection.

Stage six: what happens next? Acceptance or rejection

So you have heard back from the journal on the outcome of the reviewing process and have received the editor's decision. When there is no consensus among the reviewers as to what should happen to the paper, the editor should provide a lead. This is usually phrased something like 'I suggest that you concentrate on Reviewer A's comments.' If there is disagreement between reviewers and the editor does not give a lead, then you should contact her or him to clarify exactly what they want you to do.

Anwar received the editor's letter and reviewers' comments on a paper he had submitted to a journal special issue. The decision was that he should revise and resubmit the paper for further reviewing. When he read the reviewers' comments, he realised that the two sets of suggestions would take the paper in completely opposite directions and that he could not possibly fulfil both reviewers' requirements. However, the guest editors of the journal had not indicated to him which reviewer to focus on. When he asked what to do, he was told that he should make his own decision on this, so he followed the suggestions that were more in line with his own thinking. The resubmitted paper was sent back to the reviewers. One reviewer (and you can guess which) pronounced the paper much improved and recommended publication without further ado and as a matter of urgency because of its immediate importance. The other reviewer said that unfortunately the changes made to the paper had 'rendered it unpublishable'. Happily for Anwar, the editors decided to follow the first reviewer's opinion.

What you do once you receive a response from the journal depends upon which of the scenarios listed above your paper falls into. Let's go through each in turn.

Scenario 1, unconditional acceptance. In this case there is nothing to do at this stage except celebrate.

Scenario 2, accepted subject to minor revisions. You need to pay very close attention to what you have been asked to do and think carefully about how to respond to each suggestion. You shouldn't make compromises that make you feel uncomfortable or that you don't agree with, but you shouldn't be truculent or resistant to what may well be sensible suggestions. When you have finished the revisions, write an itemised letter to the editor setting out how you have addressed each and every request for revision. If you have declined to follow any particular revision, you need to explain in detail why.

Scenario 3, revise and resubmit. Here the suggestions are likely to be more general than specific and will undoubtedly require quite a lot of work. Again, you need to think carefully about what has been suggested and you may well need to take advice from your mentors and critical friends on how to approach the task. Again, when you have finished your rewrite, you need to construct a careful letter to the editor explaining how you have addressed the reviewers' comments. This letter will normally be sent back out to the reviewers with your revised paper. Your paper will then go through the same process as before, often being returned to the original reviewers. If you have done the job properly your next letter from the editor should be of scenario 1 or 2 type.

Scenario 4, outright rejection. You need to take a cool, long look at the reasons why your paper was rejected. It may take a little while before you feel able to do so, as you will undoubtedly feel hurt, undermined, angry or offended (or some combination of these) by the rejection. It is particularly important that you do return to your paper to see how it could best be salvaged. If you have taken our advice so far, it is likely that with sufficient effort you will be able to make a publishable paper out of it.

Having reappraised your paper in the light of the feedback you have received on it, and after taking advice from suitably experienced colleagues, you may genuinely believe that the rejection was a product of unfair reviewing, ideological conflicts or even personal animosity. In such circumstances you should send the paper, perhaps with some revision in the light of feedback, to another journal.

If, however, you realise that the paper was indeed very weak, you need to decide whether or not you can actually rescue it. This will involve you going back to the drawing board to restart the process at an appropriate point. How far back you go will depend on how bad you think your paper is and the reasons for the problems with it.

Stacey had recently completed her PhD and developed her first substantive journal paper from it. She received a crushing and ineptly worded set of brusque comments back from the reviewers and an outright rejection from the editor. In consequence, it took her a while ▶

▶ to regain her self-confidence and equilibrium. She took the paper to one of her senior colleagues, who she felt would be able to advise her. He suggested resubmitting the paper to a journal in a completely different disciplinary area where Stacey had no particular expertise, although she had called upon some of the theoretical resources of that discipline. She was uncomfortable with the advice, as it seemed to her that it did not take her or her paper seriously, was quite dismissive and had little chance of being a successful strategy. She went to another senior colleague, who spent some time helping Stacey to address the serious weaknesses in her line of argument so that she could resubmit the paper to a journal in her own disciplinary field. At the same time, she procured technical assistance from another experienced colleague who helped her address the criticisms of the statistical data in her paper. Clearly, reworking the paper at this level is taking her some time, but she has much more chance of success this way.

Stage seven: the technicalities of proofs and copyright

Once your paper has finally been accepted there will be what will probably feel like an age (and may actually be one) before anything seems to happen. Editors like to have a substantial number of accepted papers 'in the bag' in order to give themselves flexibility in putting each edition of the journal together and to save themselves nightmares about not having enough papers to publish. When things finally happen, you will be expected to act yesterday. It usually goes something like this. All of a sudden, when you are least expecting it, are about to give birth or go on holiday, you will receive printer's proofs. These are copy pages of the paper as it will appear on the page in the published journal. These days they are likely to be sent electronically as a read-only PDF file.

The editor will ask you to check the proofs for spelling errors, serious omissions of chunks of text, missing or inaccurate references, etc. If you have done your job properly up to now, you should have very little work to do at this stage unless something has gone wrong with the typesetting – unlikely but it does happen. However, you do need to proof-read very carefully and don't get so carried away with the beauty of your own prose that you miss glaring typos. Editors will be furious with you if, at this stage, you seek to make amendments (rather than typographical corrections) to the text. And rightly so – the technicalities of actually putting a journal together are immense and amendments at this stage can be financially costly. If you really do need to make an amendment it will need careful and sensitive negotiations with the editor to see if it is feasible.

Along with the proofs, you will receive a copyright assignment form. We dealt with the issue of intellectual property rights (IPR) in Chapter 3. You and any co-authors will be asked to sign the form and return it with the proofs. This form is very important, as without it the publishers will not go to press with your article in case you sue them for breach of copyright.

Both the proofs and the copyright matters need to be dealt with as a matter of urgency – usually within two or three days of receipt.

5 Publishing Books and in Books

Having dealt with journal papers in Chapter 4, we go on in this chapter to talk about publishing books and in books. We first define our subject then discuss why you might choose this publishing form and set out the practicalities of how to go about it.

What do we mean, books?

In this chapter we talk about two specific sorts of books: research monographs and edited collections (we deal briefly with textbooks in Chapter 6). Because these terms are as clear as mud, here is a brief description of the type of books we mean.

- *Research monographs.* 'Monograph' is a confusing word and we looked it up in the *Oxford English Dictionary* to resolve an argument about its meaning. It has its origins in the study of natural history, where it meant a 'treatise on one species or genus' rather than a general work that covered a number of areas. In wider usage, therefore, it means a book that is concerned with one principal theme (which may, in itself, be quite broad). You should think of it as a book with one consistent argument or set of arguments that runs through from the introduction to the conclusion and is based on research (hence 'research monograph'). It follows that one or more people may author a monograph. Occasionally, the authors may have separate chapters specifically attributed to them. Monographs may be published as part of a themed series, in which case one or more academics will edit the series. Their job is to ensure that the series as a whole has some coherence.
- *Edited collections.* As the name implies, these books are put together by an editor (or editors). The book will be, or at least profess to be, on a particular topic or theme and will include several chapters by

different authors. Each chapter will have separately attributed authorship. The editor(s) job is to give the collection coherence, and they usually reflect this by writing an introductory chapter. Editors of collections of academic writing are nearly always academics and researchers themselves.

Of course this typology isn't comprehensive. There are some less common forms of academic research publication such as when well established scholars publish collections of work that has already been published in different places. These are often called 'essay collections'.

What's in books for me?

Now that we've defined our terms, you may like to think about which book format, if any, is going to suit you. Different disciplines have different traditions with regard to books. For instance, in accounting it is quite unusual to be the author of a research monograph, whilst in history it is the prime mode of publication. The popularity of edited collections similarly varies between disciplines. Whatever the traditions in your area, your first and main consideration should be whether or not a book format is an appropriate medium in which to publish your research work. We discuss the relative merits of research monographs and edited collections below.

Research monographs

A major advantage of a monograph is that its greater length allows you to develop your ideas into a more sustained, complex and comprehensive argument than would be possible in, say, a journal paper. This is especially the case if you have a large amount of rich qualitative data or archival evidence that you need to describe and analyse.

Associated with this, books offer the advantage of a reasonable degree of flexibility in terms of their structure, approach and generic form. That is, you can often be more experimental and innovative in the way in which you approach the writing of a book, especially compared with most journal publications.

A third advantage is that books can escape the kind of territorial gatekeeping that can be associated with journal editorship. This can be especially useful if your work is somewhat less than mainstream. This is not to say that books are not subject to rigorous peer scrutiny both in the initial proposal stages, when the manuscript is submitted and after publication (that is, in reviews of the book). On the downside, publishing in books exposes your work to the sort of commercial pressures under which publishers operate and which are less in evidence in journal publication.

If you are finishing or have recently finished a higher research degree such as a doctorate, the book form offers you substantial publication at marginal cost. Don't run away with the idea that a thesis can simply be submitted to a publisher as it was examined, no matter how good it is. However, with some careful restructuring and rewriting, it may be possible to convert the one to the other relatively quickly. This can provide a substantial boost to a developing career.

Finally, writing a good and well received research monograph is undoubtedly an excellent way of firmly establishing your academic credentials and expertise in that particular area. The number of people who read journal articles is notoriously low and specialised. With a good book, you are more likely to reach a much wider audience including both academics in fields other than your own, practitioners and even interested lay people.

Edited collections

Edited collections come into existence for a number of reasons:

- One or more people at a conference (usually the organisers) may feel that some or all of the papers are of sufficient quality and hang together well enough to merit collecting them into an edited book.
- A group of people working loosely together over a period to discuss, research and develop ideas and articles may decide to collect them and publish them jointly.
- Quite often specially convened seminar series on particular themes may generate edited collections.
- An innovative thinker may decide to map out a new or developing field and do so by commissioning chapters for an edited collection.
- Research networks or teams may combine together to produce one or more edited collections based on their linked research projects.
- Major funded programmes of research, which consist of a number of parallel projects, will often result in the production of a volume

that pulls together various packages of work around the programme theme.

Of course there may be a multitude of other routes by which these books get started but we hope you've got the idea. It follows from the list above that edited collections are capable of doing quite a few different things.

- A typist transcribing one of Rebecca's research interviews heard 'research monograph' as 'research monologue'. In a way, that's what a research monograph is. By contrast, an edited collection allows a number of different voices to be heard. In good collections the chapters will 'speak to' each other, mapping or developing a field of research.
- The process of writing some edited collections can be a great way of getting authors to engage, talk and build relationships with other researchers.
- Edited collections, by virtue of the fact that the work is divided between more people, offer at least the prospect of getting the stuff out there quite quickly. That said, they also offer the opportunity for more arguments and delays caused by the bad behaviour of just one or two people.
- For those of you aspiring to promotion, being the editor of such a collection is a great way to demonstrate research leadership – if you do it well.
- For students and emerging researchers, edited collections can offer something of a panoramic view of a field without some of the intimidation that can come from starting on a pile of dense research monographs.
- Some edited collections (or research monographs) are so successful at speaking to a broad range of audiences that they come to be used in university teaching or even have courses based around them. If you ever succeed in writing or editing such a book then give yourself a pat on the back for making your research clear, accessible and influential in teaching.

All that said, edited collections are sometimes not popular with publishers. This is because edited collections can be a jumble of dislocated papers of varying quality with little internal coherence. As a result they don't sell well. Nevertheless, the best ones are very popular with both purchasers and, consequently, publishers.

Publishers, proposals and contracts

Okay, you may have got to the point where you have decided that publication in some form of book is the right thing for your work. What do you do next? It's an obvious thing to say, but books are published by publishers. This means that you have to engage with these strange beasts if you want to get a book into print. As part of the partnership there will be two key documents – a book proposal and a contract. The proposal is the document that you send to the publisher which describes your proposed book and in which you set out the case for why they should publish it. The contract is the legally binding agreement between you and the publisher concerning your book.

You need to treat writing a book as a publishing project from the outset. Your book will be a collaborative venture between you and your publisher, meaning that it is important to get a publisher on board as early on as possible. It is highly inadvisable to delay contacting publishers and obtaining a contract until your book is written. The publisher's deadlines and guidance will give you something to write to, both in terms of time and the nature of the book.

We will now consider publishers, proposals and contracts in turn.

Publishers

Publishers are people who are in business to make money. However, it would be wrong to assume that this necessarily stops them from being nice people with a commitment to the production of good books. An author's relationship with a publisher should be a genuine partnership. If you can find a publisher who has good business skills and shares your values about books then your partnership will be sound and mutually rewarding. Above all, remember that they need good authors as much as good authors need them. Try to make it a mutually advantageous and successful relationship.

That said, you will almost always have to take the lead in finding a publisher for your book and developing this relationship with them. A variation on this theme is that, sometimes, a publisher may agree to have a whole series of books around one general theme. They will appoint a series editor (who is likely to be a senior academic) who may come along and ask if you would like to contribute a book. We mention this route into publishing throughout this chapter, but here it is sufficient to note that such an invitation obviates the need to find your own publisher and slightly changes the sort of relationship that you have with them.

Publishers vary enormously in the types of books they take on and also the subject areas they choose to concentrate on. Because of the potential profits, publishers are increasingly drawn to textbooks, making research monographs and edited collections something of a niche market.

The best way to find a publisher who might be willing to take your book is to start looking at and asking about the firms that have published books in your area. The publishers will have carefully developed markets, and target their marketing and sales at these. This means that you are unlikely to be taken on if your book does not appeal to their customer base, even if your book is the best thing since the fourteen-volume boxed set on sliced bread. Whatever types of book they take, they are unlikely to want to take on a book that is a direct competitor with something they already have on their list, especially if it's fairly recent.

Publishers generally have pretty good websites and this allows easy browsing of the sorts of stuff they publish and their guidance to potential authors. You should also evaluate how 'businesslike' the publishers are: look for ones that have a good reputation for effective marketing, good 'production values' (that is, their books look good and don't fall apart quickly) and minimal production delays. Think about which publishers regularly send you good catalogues and other publicity full of things that you find interesting.

It seems to us that the current trend in publishing is for publishers to follow what they think the market is rather than try to shape it. Because profit margins are usually small in research publishing, many firms are unwilling to take risks. Some smaller, independent publishers may prioritise political or strategic aims and be less commercially oriented, but they still have to wash their own faces financially. Yet others are niche publishers, concentrating on only very limited areas (but often doing it very well). University publishing houses tend to be more keen to publish monographs but, we think, are usually less good at marketing. Think internationally when you are looking for a publisher – your book will be more acceptable to publishers if it is saleable in major international markets such as the USA and the UK. All this means that you may have a long search for a publisher who is right for you.

Once you have done this stage of your homework you can draw up a list of publishers you wish to target, and a preferred order for doing so. Here you need to flex your networking skills (see *Building Networks*) because it is important to establish human contact with them in order to try out whether they would be interested in receiving a proposal from you.

The human you need to contact is called the *commissioning editor*. Publishers have a commissioning editor for each specialist area they deal with. You should be able to get this person's name from the firm's website. These editors are usually very knowledgeable about books, journals and individual academics in their field and, we find, are generally supportive and encouraging individuals. They need to become your friend and ally if you want your book published.

Sometimes commissioning editors visit university departments. Often such visits are to search out potential textbook authors, but if they have cold-called you in your office you shouldn't feel abashed about talking to them about your research publication plans. Commissioning editors can also often be found staffing publishers' bookstalls at conferences (and giving away freebies such as pens and copies of journals). These people will be happy to talk about research monographs and edited collections – and the easy-going conference atmosphere and the fact that they are holding themselves open to approaches can make this social work seem less intimidating. Alternatively, you can establish contact by email and then possibly phone them or arrange to go to their office if this is convenient. If you are based outside the USA or UK, you will need to make strategic and well planned use of conferences and your visits to cities overseas for other purposes to add on some networking with publishers – it may be the only chance you have to meet them.

You may decide to approach a series editor (who, remember, will be an academic) with regard to your book if you feel it would fit well in their series. The same considerations apply here except that the series editor acts as an intermediary between you and the publisher. And be warned that the support of the series editor does not guarantee the book will be published. It will still have to get past 'Sales'.

Because publishers vary enormously in the sort of books they publish and the areas they cover, a rejection from one doesn't necessarily mean that you will be rejected by all of them. Often commissioning editors will give you helpful guidance – either on how to shape your proposal so that it is more likely to succeed with them, or on alternative publishers who might be more interested in your particular book.

Remember also that academic publishing is a small world, with lots of staff movement between publishing houses. Commissioning editors invariably know their counterparts in other firms and talk to them on a regular basis. This means that it is very bad form to send your proposal to more than one publisher at the same time – especially without telling them that you are doing so. It costs publishing houses real money to engage with your proposal so they would be justified in feeling rather annoyed if you were cheating on them. Enough said?

Proposals

When you have run your idea for a book by the commissioning editor and got at least a reasonably encouraging response, you need to draft the proposal. Do not underestimate the care needed in drafting this document or the amount of time it will take. A book proposal needs to be well written and to the point. You will, undoubtedly, have to go through many drafts to get it right and should get your critical friends – especially those who regularly read book proposals for publishers – to comment on it for you.

Before you start writing the proposal, make sure that you have read any guidelines that your proposed publisher has available. You will normally find these on the publisher's website. We have reproduced below the guidelines from the Sage website and expanded on each section. Nearly all publishers have similar guidelines on their websites. While you do not need to follow them slavishly, you do need to make sure that you have addressed all the questions raised in them.

Book Proposals

The following list is intended both as a guide to the points which the author(s) should consider when planning a book, and to the information which we need in order to consider a new book proposal.

Statement of Aims

Background: Please describe the background to the book (e.g. is it derived from research, practice or teaching?).

▶

It's important to make an early impact with this section. You need to establish the absolute cutting-edge importance of what your book is about and the likelihood of it being good by setting out its provenance in solid research by reputable researchers. Don't say something like 'I've been thinking about this for a while and thought I might have a go at writing it up ...' *Do* say something like 'This book arises from a major government-funded research project conducted over the past three years ...'

If the proposed book is based on your PhD, you need to approach these explanations with some care. Publishers tend to be very wary of taking on PhD theses as books, largely because so many academics think that all they have to do is send in their thesis and it will be published as it stands. You should reappraise your doctoral research as if it were a regular stand-alone research project – which it is, but you won't be used to thinking about it like that.

Rationale: A brief description of the rationale behind the proposal. What are the book's main themes and objectives?

In this section you need to explain carefully why your proposed book will be worth buying and reading. Publishers need to know that there is a market for their books. For academic books, this means that you have to address pertinent and relevant issues in a rigorous and interesting way. You are trying to convince the commissioning editor that your proposed book passes the 'so what?'-ness test. In doing this, you will be laying good foundations for the arguments that you will make later in the proposal about the book's wide appeal.

Approach: Description and reasons for the approach adopted.

Your rationale for the book must run seamlessly into your description of how you will tackle the shaping and writing of it. For example, you may be interested in theoretical questions about national identity and approach them through a case study of constructions of Irishness and the consumption of Guinness. You need to make the links between the aims and objectives of your book and the way in which you have tackled the subject explicit and irrefutably logical. You also need to describe the way in which the book would be constructed and what the logic of that is.

▶ Features: What aspects of this proposal would you emphasise as being of most importance? Are there any deliberate omissions? Any other features you would like taken into account.

This is the key place in which you can highlight the unique selling points of your book. What makes it original? What would draw people into reading it? We all have our favourite books for certain purposes and usually recommend them to others with comments such as 'If you want to understand that, you can't do better than read Jones' book ...' At the same time, don't make claims for your proposed book that are plainly over-ambitious.

Definition of Market

This is an important section for publishers because they need to know if there will be a sufficiently broad market for your book and where to direct their marketing campaign if they publish it. Academic books seldom achieve mass popular readership, though sometimes academics write popular books. For instance, Stephen Hawking, a Cambridge theoretical physicist, would not get near the best-seller market with his regular academic work, but his *Brief History of Time*, written for the lay person, has been a runaway sales success. When was the last time you picked up an academic book at the airport for a long-haul flight? This means that the market for your book will be confined to people within your own academic discipline and possibly those related to it. The better theorised your work is, the more likely it is to appeal to a wider range of academic disciplines. There are a number of texts that are read across a wide range of disciplines despite their apparently narrow subject base.

If you work in an area which involves practice (for example, teaching) you may also have a practitioner audience. But bear in mind that writing well for both academics and practitioners simultaneously is very difficult. Be wary of falling between two stools.

Readership: Who is the book primarily aimed at? Who will buy it? Who will read it? Would this subject have international appeal? If so, where? Is the subject area of the proposal widely taught? ▶

▶ Level: What level of ability is assumed of the reader (undergraduate/postgraduate/prequalifying/postqualifying etc.)? To what level does the book take the reader?

Now that you have defined the broad market for your book, you need to make some detailed arguments about exactly which people are likely to read and buy your book and why. For instance, you may have identified that your market is among academic and practising lawyers but you now need to be able to say whether they will be undergraduate students or fellow academics, whether they will be corporate lawyers or family lawyers, and in which countries. Be quite realistic about the level of existing knowledge people will need in order to understand your book. Don't claim that it's for first-year undergraduates when you know that PhD students might find it hard. You must define the benefits of your book for your target audiences.

Existing Books

Which existing books in the area are closest to your proposal and how do they compare? Is there a clear competitor?

In responding, it's no good leaving out your book's main competitors in the hope that the commissioning editor has never heard of them – they invariably have an intimate knowledge of the market in which they work. If you don't mention key texts in the area, you will come over as someone who is uninformed and therefore not a reliable author. Whilst they won't want to enter a saturated market, they can be quite hesitant about publishing 'into a void'. So address existing texts and explain the ways in which your book can complement, extend or challenge or otherwise be distinguished from them.

Detailed synopsis

Outline: Provisional list of contents and working title, including chapter headings and subheadings and paragraph-length chapter descriptions explaining what you intend to cover in each chapter.

▶

▶ This is an extremely important part of your proposal. You need to use it to convince the publisher that you know what you are about, that your book has a good structure and flow, and that it makes sense. You will need to write a short abstract for each chapter and give them good titles. While chapter headings are essential, it is probably not necessary to provide subheadings for a research monograph at this point. Taken as a whole, the synopsis must summarise the story that you are trying to tell in your book in a lively and interesting fashion.

Length: Estimated overall length including references and footnotes, often best arrived at by assigning lengths to each chapter.

Because of technical production constraints and the need to keep the price of books to what the market will bear (longer books cost more), publishers will usually define the minimum and maximum length of books. Check on the publisher's website for details of the lengths of books that they will countenance. As a rough guide, a short book will be around 60,000 words, a standard one 80,000 and a long one 100,000. The length needs to be appropriate to both your subject matter and the target readership.

Timetable

This is a very fraught point. Academic work loads across the world tend to be excessive, and delivering a book to publishers on time becomes increasingly difficult in consequence. At the same time, publishers are becoming increasingly tetchy with academic authors who don't deliver their manuscript within a reasonable time. This is entirely understandable. Publishing houses are businesses and have to produce catalogues, plan production schedules and marketing campaigns and maintain the value of their 'brand' by producing a continuous, steady stream of high-quality texts. You are their suppliers and if you let them down, like any business, they will suffer. There is no easy answer here. However, you can make things easier by setting realistic timetables. If you find that you are falling seriously behind schedule, most publishers will understand, provided you keep them informed. They ▶

are generally committed to your book once they have commissioned it – it costs them money to commission a book (for example, staff time and free copies or payment to academic readers of the proposal) so they won't give up on you lightly. Our commissioning editor for *ASK* told us that among recent, quite credible, reasons she'd been given for late submission of manuscripts were a ceiling falling down in a university and, in another instance, somebody being temporarily deafened by a dynamite explosion in Guatemala. *C'est la vie.*

> Are any chapters available in draft form? When would you be able to make some available?

If you've already drafted some chapters for the book, you should enclose them, indicating their stage of development. However, it is not advisable to send a publisher your PhD or any part of it. Writing for publication and writing a thesis are two quite distinct genres and they can't be used interchangeably. If you don't have any draft chapters, the chances are that you will have one or more journal papers or reports relevant (at least tangentially) to the proposed book. It is a good idea to send one or two of these to the publisher simply to show that you are able to write coherently and also to give an indication of the intended nature of the book. It may be that you will use a journal paper as the basis of one of your chapters. If so, you should say so.

> Illustrations: How many tables, diagrams or illustrations will there be (roughly)?

Publishers are very wary of production costs. If you are, for instance, an art historian or write about visual culture, you may well want colour plates. These can be very expensive to print and publishers will need the issue to be flagged up well in advance so that they can factor it in to their costings and pricing decisions.

If you want to reproduce anything that might be held under someone else's copyright (for example, statistical tables or visual images) it needs to be flagged up here too. Publishers usually require authors to obtain the necessary permissions. This may involve payments on your part, so factor that in to your own budget.

▶ ## *Additional Information*

> About you: Please make sure you supply correct details of full name, position, address, telephone number, e-mail where available, together with brief details of other posts, degrees, relevant qualifications, publications (with any books indicated), and nationality.

Publishers don't need your full CV here. Nor do they necessarily need information about all the courses you teach or the university committees that you sit on. They need a short and relevant CV. For more guidance on how to do CVs see *Building your Academic Career*.

We are unsure why a publisher may need to know your nationality. It may be because it can affect matters such as the payment of royalties, and the British Library and the Library of Congress will eventually need the information for cataloguing your book. It may also be that the larger international firms of publishers like to let each branch deal with people in their own geographical area. You certainly shouldn't think that your nationality will affect the likelihood of your proposal being accepted.

> Referees: Please supply the names and addresses of several people whom you would regard as suitably qualified to comment on the proposal.

You do not necessarily have to know the people you name as referees personally, but it is good to know something about them. It's not a good idea to select someone with a reputation for being cutting and destructive about other people's work. You should ask friends, mentors and doctoral supervisors for advice on this. It's generally good practice to send an email to the people you want to name asking them if they are happy about it. Naming referees from more than one country is also a good idea, as it demonstrates that your work can travel.

> Supporting Material: Do you have any material which you would regard as an adequate indication of the book's level and content: draft chapters, lecture notes, journal articles etc.? We

▶

> ▶ may need to see draft chapters before reaching a final decision on acceptance.
>
> We have written above about draft chapters and journal articles. The same things apply here. If you have something in reasonably good shape, it's sensible to send it with an indication of the relationship it has to your final book manuscript. What you send does not have to be in its polished, final form. Publishers know they are drafts but want an indication of your style, approach and abilities. However, don't send the publisher writing that is scrappy or unintelligible to anyone except yourself.

Once you've polished your proposal, you need to send it to your targeted commissioning editor. If you've prepared the ground thoroughly, they will be expecting your proposal and will send it out to readers, who are usually well established academics working in your field, some of whose names you may have suggested. This part of the process can take some time, as invariably the readers of book proposals will be busy people.

If the referees' comments are favourable and the publisher is quite interested in your proposal, you may have to enter a period of negotiation over the precise nature and shape of the book. It's important to be both flexible and persuasive in such negotiations. Remember that yours and the publisher's best interests are served by producing the best possible book and that publishers will have considerably more experience and expertise on matters such as what will sell than you are likely to. This doesn't mean that you have to agree to everything the publisher suggests, but you must enter into a professional dialogue in which everyone respects the other's experience and expertise.

If your proposal is ultimately rejected then you need to learn the lessons from this process, incorporate any useful feedback from referees and find a different publisher. Remember that rejection may not be a consequence of a poor proposal, it may be that the proposed book was just not right for that particular publisher. If so, they might be able to point you in the direction of a suitable alternative firm. If you are ultimately completely unsuccessful in finding a publisher you might consider turning your work into a series of refereed journal articles instead.

Contracts

Contracts are binding legal agreements between you and the publisher. They set out the terms on which the book will be released. These terms should include matters such as:

- The format of the book, for example hardback, softback or both and the number of copies to be printed in the first print run. This is an important matter. Some publishers usually produce hardback and softback editions simultaneously. This is advantageous to the author because hardback books are much more expensive to buy and consequently sales of them are low. Other publishers, who make their financial margins on copies sold to libraries, tend to be predisposed to producing only a hardback edition on the first print run unless they are absolutely convinced that paperback sales will be significant. Think about these things when targeting a publisher and engaging with them.
- Copyright matters. This is a very important matter. In signing a contract you are giving the publisher the right to economically exploit your work in return for royalty payments. We dealt with IPR at some length in Chapter 3.
- Needless to say, you should pay careful attention to financial matters especially if you think that the book is likely to be a runaway best-seller. The contract will lay down the basis on which you will be paid royalties for your book, including any advance. It will specify the percentage of net profit that you will receive from sales of copies of the book and other sales of rights. It is a good idea to negotiate a differential rate depending on the number of copies sold, so that you get a higher rate once the sales of your book exceed a certain number (usually 2,000 or 3,000 copies).
- One of the most vexed issues that the contract will address is the date for the delivery of your finished typescript to your publishers. It is reasonable for publishers to need to know when to expect your manuscript. They need to plan their complicated production schedules, marketing and so on and produce reliable catalogues.
- The contract will undoubtedly specify the form that your typescript must be delivered to the publishers in and also some form of wording about it being to an acceptable standard and within spitting distance of what you promised in your proposal. The publisher usually reserves the right not to publish if you are deemed to be in breach of such undertakings.

- Other stuff the contract is likely to include are matters such as who decides what goes on the jacket, the rights to produce further editions and who will produce and maintain any websites associated with the book. The contract is also likely to specify that you will be personally liable if you libel someone. Be careful about what you're getting into.

It goes without saying that you should read the contract carefully, ask about anything you don't understand or are not happy with and think about showing it to the appropriate person in your university if there is anything you are not sure about.

Writing and editing

The beauty of having a good proposal, whether it is for an edited collection or a research monograph, is that, like a research proposal (see *Getting Started on Research*), it gives you a clear route map of how to proceed with your work. The approach needed and the work involved for research monographs differs somewhat from that required for edited collections. We'll deal with each in turn.

Writing research monographs

Whilst research monographs are a particular generic form, the points we made earlier in Chapters 2, 3 and 4 hold for writing books. If it's a while since you read those, you might like to refresh your memory on these points. In addition, there are some further considerations you need to address in writing your book.

- It may sound obvious, but a research monograph is a *monograph* – a book around a particular theme. This means that you need to be particularly careful to achieve coherence from start to finish of your book. Don't try to tell too many stories or introduce too many themes in one book. Give the poor reader the clear impression of moving through a seamless but developing argument.
- Authoring a book is undoubtedly a very substantial and complex project. If you have written a doctoral thesis you will have experience of such sustained writing and will know that you need

to plan, set yourself milestones, be well organised and generally keep yourself on course.

- Think about how you will get sufficient 'joined up' time to get this complex writing done and do not underestimate the amount of mental energy and emotional commitment needed. You cannot fit the activity in to 'the odd hour' here and there. Plan ahead: you may be able to get a sabbatical or other paid leave from regular teaching or administration work or you might decide to timetable your writing in student vacations. You will need to liaise with any co-author(s) on such timetables.

- End details are important. Think about style as you go along and be consistent. This is easier to do from the start than to have to do a huge retrospective edit for style. 'Cite while you write': trying to compile a bibliography at the end of a complex piece of writing is likely to drive you mad and almost inevitably leads to errors and omissions. Early on in the process the publisher will either send you a hard copy of their style guidelines or ask you to look at them on their website. The best way to deal with this is to adapt your writing and formatting to the relevant style from the beginning.

We're aware that a number of people reading this book will have a doctoral thesis that they are thinking of turning into a book. As we've already intimated, books and theses are different beasts and achieving the transition from one to the other merits a special note here. The key difference between the two genres is that the thesis demonstrates your competence as a researcher and scholar. The focus is, therefore, on how the study was conceived, designed and conducted. By implication, if you have done this well, the thesis will be a contribution to knowledge. The writing that you do is the story of how you conducted the study and how that resulted in a contribution to knowledge.

In contrast, the emphasis in a book lies in the knowledge itself, and the story of the study (for instance, the techniques used) is of secondary importance, there to give legitimacy to the knowledge claims made. This makes a thesis quite unsuitable for publication as a research mono-graph as it stands. That said, if you have a thesis, you will have a substantial, well thought out, well structured and theorised research document that you can quite possibly revise into monograph format by shifting the emphasis of the writing.

One of the key things you need to do is to think about the difference between the readership of the two documents. Your thesis will be read by very few people (chiefly your supervisors/advisers and examiners) and for a very specialised purpose (to pass an examination). In contrast, the audience for your book will be much more diverse and have a range of motivations. They will not necessarily be specialists in your field and they certainly won't be formally examining you. This means that the close scrutiny given to a thesis is never accorded a book. There are two principal implications for you as a writer.

First, in a thesis the golden rule is 'if in doubt, leave it in', as you need to make sure that all your knowledge claims are comprehensively and reliably justified. The fact that in the UK the oral examination is often referred to as a 'defence' of the thesis gives an indication of the imperatives in this regard. In contrast, with a book the golden rule is 'if in doubt, leave it out'. You do no kindness to the reader of a book by bludgeoning them with data and references, forcing them to wade through a morass of justificatory evidence. Of course, this is no excuse for sloppy scholarship or unfounded assertions rather than rigorous arguments – it's all a matter of balance and judgement.

Second, whereas there are certain necessary elements in a thesis, such as a detailed description of the methodology, historiography or whatever, these may not be relevant or appropriate in book format. Conversely, you may have material or case studies or other evidence that you decided to omit from your thesis but which would fit well into your book.

Writing for and editing collections

Writing for and editing collections is a very different sort of work from writing journal papers or monographs. In this section we talk first about writing for and then about editing collections. If you are a comparatively inexperienced researcher then you are more likely to be involved in writing than in editing.

Invitations to contribute to edited collections tend to be a product of good networking (see *Building Networks*), producing polished conference papers, working collaboratively with others, attending seminars and workshops and in general making sure that you avail yourself of every sensible opportunity to participate in the wider academic community. Consequently, if you do become involved in an edited collection, it's important to demonstrate all the attributes of a good colleague. This means that you will:

- Do things on time – or, if you can't, let the editor know in plenty of time and explain why you have been delayed.
- Treat any guidance and support you get as constructive criticism and respect the fact that editors have a tough job in turning what can initially be a disparate set of chapters into a coherent book. Different editors will have very different styles and approaches to the task. Some will be very 'hands on' and interventionist, whilst others will be happy to let you do your own thing. Generally, the best interests of the editor (producing the best possible book) will coincide with your own best interests (producing the best possible chapter). Through their interventions, editors can often considerably improve your chapter and you should not just reject their interventions on principle or because you feel precious about your writing.

That said, conflicts can arise, and you should not allow yourself to be pushed into changing your chapter in ways that you really don't feel comfortable with. It can often be worth asking the opinion of a friendly third party on such matters before you go off and give vent to your rage or cave in to such demands.

Peggy is a successful research student, who was invited to submit a paper that she had given at a conference as a chapter for a book. She wrote the chapter and her supervisors read and commented on it before she sent it off to the editor.

The editor sent the chapter out to a referee and eventually returned it to Peggy with comments and proposed changes that would have substantially altered the meaning of the chapter. Peggy felt strongly that she did not want to make such changes. She discussed this with her supervisors, who advised her that she was absolutely right in her judgement.

She wrote to the editor explaining that she was not prepared to make the changes requested and withdrawing her chapter. She then slightly revised the writing for submission to the leading international journal in her field and it was accepted with only minor revisions. As an extra bonus, under the UK research evaluation system, her work 'counts' for more as a journal article than it would have done as a book chapter.

- When writing, keep in your mind the brief that your editor has given you and remember that it was drawn up in order to make the collection hang together.
- Above all, treat the endeavour of an edited collection as a collaborative effort among peers. Don't be a *prima donna*.

The advice we gave above when talking about journal articles on matters such as copyright, proofs and royalties all hold here too. Remember, also, that a chapter in a book makes you one of the publisher's 'authors' and, as such, you will normally be entitled to a discount in price on any books you buy from them. Over a period, such benefits are likely to exceed any payment you receive for your own writing.

If you are experienced, or have the reliable support of a more experienced colleague, you may decide that you will undertake the project of editing a collected book. You might do this on your own, with someone else or as part of a team. It may seem that editing a book is relative easy, but that is a delusion. Putting together a good edited collection, one that publishers will want and that people will read, is hard work – although it can also be fun. Successful editors are generally proactive, diplomatic and persistent, and tend to be good at net-working, bringing people together and academic research leadership in general. If you don't feel that you are ready for that sort of work on your own, or with the support of others, then think carefully before embarking on it.

There are several stages in the process of editing a book that you need to think about. We set them out below in order to help you formulate your own plan. Good planning at this stage can save many future heart and head aches.

Developing the concept

We dealt with the question of how such books get conceived above. But there are other issues here too. First, are there a sufficient number of suitably qualified and willing authors to write the chapters? You will need to identify and recruit suitable potential authors and you may have to be innovative and imaginative in how you do so. You may have to negotiate with them and sometimes even persuade them that the idea is a good one. You shouldn't be afraid to approach people you don't know personally. If you are writing to 'famous' people in the field, you could also ask them if they know others who might make a good contribution. In other words, recruiting authors will stretch and test your networking skills. Edited collections are a good opportunity for established and 'new' authors to have conversations in print. Don't be snobbish and only want the big names. Indeed, inexperienced authors, given suitable help and guidance, can be reliable and often extremely interesting – after all, they may need a good publication and have no laurels to rest on.

Second, is there a publisher who is likely to want to publish the book? As we said above, it is advisable to contact the commissioning editors of different publishers and talk to them about your ideas. You may have to work hard at selling them an edited collection – they may have had bitter experience of edited books that include one or two excellent chapters but are otherwise unremarkable or even boring. One thing that you will have to convince them of is that a research monograph would not be able to do the job better than your edited one. The publisher will also need to feel confident that enough of the authors are sufficiently committed to the project to make it viable, and of your own ability and determination to pull everything together.

Third, do you have the personal resources (time, energy, skills, etc.) to undertake the task? If you don't, or you are not in a position to develop them sufficiently quickly, is there somebody else that you could work with who will have complementary abilities?

If you can answer these questions positively then you are ready to go on to the next stage.

Engaging the authors

Once you've thought about the concept for the book, you need a brief outline description of what the book will be about. You can then use it both in your discussions with publishers and also to approach potential authors. Busy people, who may not prioritise the writing of book chapters, are more likely to be persuaded of the merits of your project if they are given a pithy and striking overview of what it is about. You have to sell yourself and your ideas if you want people to do work for you.

There are, obviously, many routes to finding contributors to your collection. The route you choose will often depend on the origins of the project. For instance, if it arises out of an existing research team or network, then locating a pool of authors should be less problematic than if your project arises out of a desire to pull together authors in an emerging field.

Once you have located a suitable group, you will need to check out whether they have something appropriate to contribute at this time, what their likely time scales are and whether these will work with your own. Remember that you and your authors are quite likely to need more time than you or they anticipate. You need to ask each author for an abstract. If you don't already know their writing then it's a good idea to ask them to give you quite a detailed abstract and possibly look at some of their other writing. If the potential author is an unpublished PhD student you might, for instance, ask to see an appropriate chapter from their thesis.

Of course, your interest in the topic is likely to be such that you will have important things to say in your own name and you will probably want to include a chapter on your own research work (as distinct from the introduction that you will write to the whole book). If you do this, it's important that you, as an author, are subject to the same kind of editorial processes as other contributors. If you are working with others to edit the book, then this is easily achieved by getting your fellow editors to do such work on your own chapter. If, however, you are sole editor, you should probably engage the services of a critical friend with expertise in the field.

When looking at the abstracts of potential chapters, you need to think about the overall shape of the collection and how it will all hang together. Think about connecting themes that will run through the volume. This work is necessary preparation for the introduction that you will have to write and also for writing the book proposal.

Writing the proposal

The work you've done to date in developing the concept, identifying potential authors, getting abstracts from them and thinking about how their work fits together places you in an excellent position to write a proposal to send to a possible publisher of your book. Everything that we said about book proposals above holds here.

Organising authors = herding cats

Once you have your authorial team in place and a contract for the book, your hard work really begins. Your job as the editor is to manage the process in such a way that you achieve your goal. How you do this will depend on factors such as your own style and personality and those of the particular authors you have on board and the type of book it is. You need to be flexible and adaptive in this work: don't try to be highly interventionist with someone who is very senior, willing and capable.

Formally you will be responsible for organising legal matters such as the contract and also for setting out a time scale for the production of the book. When you send people the notional timetable you need to allow for slippage. It is very rare for everyone to be able to produce exactly to time. Wily editors know this and may set deadlines for authors well ahead of the actual ones.

The type of book you are editing will shape the organisation that's needed for its production. For instance, if you decide *ex ante* that you will produce a book from an intended seminar series, then somebody has to organise the meetings and make sure that the speakers understand what is required of them. Alternatively, if a good conference leads you to decide to pull a selection of the papers together into a book, the management task may be limited to co-ordinating the return of polished papers. In short, think about the tasks to be done in terms of the nature of the project and plan well ahead.

Editing the chapters

Invariably, the chapters of your collection will come to you in various stages of readiness. Whilst some will be wonderfully written, more often they will need careful editorial attention. Review them with two things in mind. First, does the chapter work as a coherent argument in its own right and is it well written? Your suggestions for improvement must be constructive and, if you want major changes, then you need to be both diplomatic and detailed in your feedback.

Sometimes a piece of writing will come in and it will be a horror story. You should give detailed and constructive feedback and give the author(s) at least one opportunity to get it right. If it comes back and is still unacceptable, then you may decide that the book really doesn't need it and reject it politely. If you do this, you should, however, give further detailed feedback to the author(s). If the topic of the chapter is crucial to the integrity of the book, you can either substantially rewrite it yourself or persuade an alternative author whom you are confident in to contribute a chapter on the topic.

Rosa and Gertrude were editing a book that was likely to be extremely important and influential in their area. The chapter they received from one key contributor was wholly unacceptable. However, the book would be seriously weakened if it did not address the issues raised in it. They felt they had no alternative but to substantially rewrite it themselves. This required careful negotiation with the original author and the editors, in the interests of diplomacy, decided to leave his name alone on the piece. The book was subsequently very influential and the rewritten chapter became one of the most frequently cited pieces from the book. The original author, sadly, used his supposed sole authorship of the chapter to his career advantage.

The second question to ask yourself when reviewing the piece is whether it fits with the themes and remit of the book as a whole. If it is problematic in this regard, you may want to remind the authors to look back at the proposal to the publisher, which you will have sent them at the outset and which will have included all the abstracts.

Feedback should be multilateral. That is, it should not be confined to a dialogue between you and each individual author. All the authors need to know about important themes and developments in others' work so that they can reflect (and reflect on) them in their own drafts. You may well want, with the authors' permission, to circulate drafts to all or selected contributors or to put particular authors in touch with each other in order to facilitate this process. Where it is practical, you may want to organise a day to 'workshop' the chapters once first drafts are in.

Pulling it all together

As the chapters start to be assembled in their final format, you need to think about the editorial writing that you will do to wrap them all up together. There are a number of ways of doing this and you will have to judge what is the most appropriate for your book. You may decide simply to have a detailed introduction that lays out the themes of the following chapters and explains what is to come. In addition, you may have decided (and proposed to the publishers) that the book should have a final chapter written by the editor(s) that explicates, develops and theorises the individual contributions. When you lay out your time scales you must remember that you won't be able to do this complicated work until you have all the first drafts in.

Delivery and deliverance

Your final task as editor is to get the manuscript into the format designated by the publisher. As with research monographs, you will have the publisher's style sheets from the publisher. This may appear to be a small matter of detail, but it is vitally important that you deliver a manuscript that complies as closely as possible with these stylistic guidelines.

A way of saving yourself huge amounts of rather mundane and tedious work at this stage is to ensure that you get hold of the publisher's style guidance early in the process and send it to your authors. You can then politely require them to ensure that their own chapters are produced in the appropriate form. This means that your job becomes one of checking rather than reformatting – as you hope, though it doesn't always happen like that. You should also ask your authors to put their manuscripts into whatever font you are working in, as you should send a good-looking manuscript in, not one that looks like a dog's breakfast.

Ensuring a happy ending

Whether you've written a monograph or edited a collection, the process once the manuscript is in its final form is essentially the same. If you want your book to be published quickly and with good production quality, then you need to continue to play your part promptly and efficiently. This is what will happen:

Looking good

You need to send the publisher a hard copy (sometimes two) and an electronic copy of the whole book, in the style that they have asked for, with pages numbered appropriately and so on. We cannot over-emphasise the importance of making the text as good and consistent as you possibly can.

Readers' comments

Sometimes your book will be sent out for readers' comments at this stage. This will have been made clear to you at the contract stage. If this is the case, then you may be asked to make some revisions to content or approach and you will then have to respond to the suggestions made. You should look back at what we said above about responding to referees' comments on journal articles to help you with this.

Copy editing

All books will be subject to copy editing. Copy editors read for things like the formatting of the manuscript, diagrams, grammar, spelling, punctuation, clarity of meaning and the accuracy of citations and references. Sometimes they will return the whole manuscript to you with their comments and a letter asking you to look at particular pages and queries. Often they will send you only the pages on which they have suggested alterations.

Whichever, when you get the manuscript back, you will need to respond to their comments and queries quickly but being extremely careful in the way you review the proposed changes. Copy editors are not experts in your field and sometimes they may propose alterations that inadvertently change the meaning of what you have written.

If you are editing a collection, you should ask contributing authors to check their own copy-edited articles, but beware of the slow response. Make sure that you give authors a firm deadline for returning their comments to you and that they know that, whether you have heard from them or not, you will be replying to the copy editor by a particular date. The fact that you have sent copy to individual authors does not excuse you, as editor, from your responsibility for checking the copy editing of all the chapters, so do it for the whole book regardless of what you send to your contributors.

Covering yourself

Although you are not supposed to judge a book by its cover, most people do. It is therefore very important to pay careful attention to what your finished book as a 'product' is going to look like on the shelves. You should be able to negotiate the type of cover with the publisher. If you have seen books in their catalogue that have a particularly good cover you should tell your editor, as it will enable them to commission the same designer. Bear in mind, though, that if you wish to use a photograph, original artwork or anything else which might carry somebody's copyright, then you will need to ensure that you have the necessary copyright clearance (and this might involve paying a fee).

Once the publisher has the manuscript and has accepted it, they will then commission a cover design. Publishers will often send you a few (maybe three or four) possible covers for your comments. Again, you need to respond as quickly and constructively as possible. It won't help the publisher if you just say that you hate that cover without saying why. If your book is one of a series, your cover will follow the series design, though it is likely that there will be some room for individuality within it.

In nearly all cases, you will be asked to provide the cover 'blurb' – the text for the back of the book. This text will also be replicated in the publisher's catalogue, other publicity materials and on e-booksellers' websites. It is therefore important that it is both accurate and enticing for the reader.

Once the cover design has been finalised, the publisher will send you 'proofs' (that is, an exact version of what the final thing will look like on the page) of your cover. This will require your careful attention, as it will also include the blurb and also any information, usually about yourself, that will go on the inside flaps of any dust jacket. You may also have been asked by the publisher to provide them with the names of reputable commentators in your field who might be willing to be quoted on the back of your book and in other publicity material.

Page proofs

At about the same time as you get possible covers, you are likely to be sent the page proofs of your book for proof reading. Publishers like to produce proofs that are as close as is reasonably practicable to the final printed product. Their chief concerns will be to ensure that the pagination of the text is not altered at this stage – inserting a paragraph, or even a sentence, on page 17 of a 200 page book may create 183 consequential page changes. This is very costly and if you insist on such changes at that stage the publisher may charge you for the extra work caused. This is, therefore, definitely not the time to make final revisions. But it is your last chance to ensure that there are no errors in the final text. Publishers have standard codes and symbols for each change that you might want to make (such as deletions, insertions, spelling corrections, the use of upper or lower case) and they will be able to supply you with a list of them or direct you to where you can find them. Use them, as it avoids confusion in making the corrections.

Indexes

Once you have the page proofs, you will also need to get the index sorted out. Usually, publishers will offer you the choice of doing the index yourself or commissioning a professional indexer. If you choose the latter, the payment to the indexer will come out of your royalties.

There are advantages and disadvantages both to doing the index yourself and to getting a professional to do it. If you do it yourself, you can ensure that you have a proper index that reflects what you judge to be the key themes, topics and issues in the book. Like copy editors, indexers are seldom experts in your field so they can't necessarily make judgements about the importance of particular themes as easily or accurately as you can. However, it is also a very time-consuming task to do yourself and you will be slower than a professional.

If you choose to do your own index, you cannot rely on technology to do it for you. Computer programmes can find words and phrases but they can't make important decisions for you. For example, they can't judge whether the same concept is carried through several successive pages or not. Neither can they identify a concept if the phrase you have given the computer doesn't appear in that exact form. Often publishers will have guidelines about how they like an index to be compiled. If they do, make sure you follow their advice.

One method for doing an index

Start by making a copy of your page proofs to mark up as soon as you get them for doing your proof reading.

Read through the manuscript highlighting the words and phrases that you want to have in the index and make a note on a separate electronic file or on a card of the word/phrase/name and page number as you go. Make sure that each time you come across something that is a subdivision of something else, you make a note of both the main category and the sub-category and, if necessary, any cross-referencing needed (for example, 'Bourdieu: cultural capital' and/or 'cultural capital: Bourdieu'). You need to know in advance how many sub-categories you will use. Usually it is best not to use too many. One main category and one sub-category are probably enough.

Once you have been right through the book, sort the list into alphabetical order. If you have done the list on cards you will need to put it into electronic form at this point. If you have made an electronic file you will now need to ensure that you haven't repeated words unnecessarily.

At this point your index will be a list that looks something like a regular book index.

Some books have an index of authors and a separate index for content, themes and so on. Make sure you keep them separate if that is the case.

Selling it

Publishers take different lengths of time to actually produce the book, but while it is in production is the right time to talk with their marketing people about how best to launch and sell it. You will need to give them a list of journals to which you think it should be sent for review and any particular individuals who would be in a position to review it (and you think would review it favourably). They will also send you a marketing questionnaire (probably much earlier on) and although this is boring, you need to respond to it helpfully.

And finally ...

We think it's important to be proactive in making sure that as many people as possible know about your book and also that you celebrate the very real achievement that it represents. So think carefully about your personal marketing. Look for opportunities to distribute flyers about your book. Ask your publisher if they can produce postcards showing the cover of your book that you can send out to friends and colleagues. And you should consider having a launch event – a nice party at which those you invite can meet the authors and have an opportunity to buy the book. If there is a suitable conference coming up, you might suggest to your publisher that they organise a launch as part of the conference. Some conferences have 'book sessions' at which authors of new books are able to talk about them. Another way of launching a book is by organising a seminar or workshop based on the publication.

6 Other Sorts of Publishing

This chapter is about the other sorts of publishing that you can do as an academic. We look briefly in turn at textbooks and a whole range of alternatives to journals and research books.

Do they really matter?

While many of these other sorts of publishing do not 'count' in research audits, they may be worth doing for other reasons, such as disseminating your work to wider audiences. However, our advice would be to make sure you get the academic research publications under your belt before you turn to these other kinds of publishing. It will be better for your academic career and we also believe that the best academic writing for lay audiences and undergraduates is usually by people who are good scholars and researchers in their own right.

Textbooks and other writing for students

The massification of undergraduate education across the globe has generated an explosion in the volume and number of textbooks published. Textbooks that are produced solely and exclusively for the student (and teacher) market are easily identifiable as such and are not research publications, even though the authors frequently are accomplished academicians and researchers.

There is enormous pressure from publishers to write such books because, quite simply, they are in business and they need to publish books that will have the highest volume of sales. This is particularly the case for those courses that regularly enrol large numbers of students. If your textbook is adopted for a first-year core course that regularly has several hundred students (or, even better, for several such courses) sales will be well in excess of the usual sales of academic books and both you and your publisher will benefit financially as a result. Beware. Although encouragement may be flattering, and some people make a lot of money from writing (and annually updating) textbooks, remember that it will not count as research publication when it comes to applying for jobs, promotion or when your 'research output' is being evaluated.

There are textbooks that are very well done, extremely interesting and use excellent pedagogic devices. Such books can make a significant contribution to your own teaching and that of others and are deservedly popular. Writing a book like that can also be a good way of ensuring that you are up to speed across a broad range of topics in your field. In that way, they can help with your own pedagogic practice and perhaps even your future research. If you do decide to write a textbook, you need to make sure that you produce one like that.

The down side of the exploding market in textbook production is that many of them are of quite poor quality and uninformed by excellent scholarship or good research. If you are an emerging academic researcher and a relatively inexperienced teacher you are unlikely to be in a good position to write a good (or even a fair to middling) textbook. Anything less than a good textbook is highly unlikely to do anything to enhance your academic career and reputation. Furthermore, while you are writing it, you won't be doing the research and other academic writing that will build your reputation.

If you and your colleagues run a successful course that attracts significant numbers of students (either at your own institution or across your sector), it might be worth considering turning your course material into a textbook. Although you can do so at marginal cost, that cost may still be significant. However, it would encourage you to address pedagogical issues in a coherent and systematic way, enhance the reputation of your department in that area of teaching (thus attracting more and better students) and even make a tidy profit for you and/or your institution. (In the UK, at least, universities usually claim the copyright in course materials).

Quite often, 'textbooks' are now multimedia events and authors find themselves not only producing the text but also guidance notes for tutors to accompany them (sometimes with model 'answers' to examples or questions if appropriate), CD-ROMs, blackboard material, websites and so on. Whilst writing textbooks can be lucrative, you need to be aware that you may also be obliged to produce such additional material, which, especially in the case of a website, may require constant updating. This can add up to a considerable amount of work without actually adding to your career prospects, list of publications or income.

One form of textbook that can be easier to produce, show greater synergies with research and become popular is the 'reader'. A reader may include book chapters or articles, whole or in part, specially commissioned new chapters, journalistic pieces, pieces of legislation or court reports, archival documents, photographs and so on. They should be carefully selected to map a whole field, to introduce students to an area or to highlight particularly salient issues. Whichever of these it is, you will need to write a commentary that links the pieces you have chosen together. This commentary may take the form of an extended introduction to the whole book, or to a particular part of the book, or it may be a narrative woven through all the pieces. In the UK, the Open University (a large distance learning institution) is renowned for its production of high-quality readers.

Dictionaries, encyclopaedias, reference books and annotated bibliographies

These types of book are many and varied. Some of them are a snare and a delusion, but others are invaluable to academics, postgraduate and undergraduate students. Most academics will have at least some of these books on their shelves and often recommend them to students. Libraries tend to be keen purchasers of such books. We say a few words about some of the main forms of this genre below.

Dictionaries and encyclopaedias

Academic dictionaries are only a distant relation of the type of book used for the definition of words in any particular language. Because they deal with concepts, writers, events, legislation, schools of thought, literature, etc., the entries tend to be more expansive and discursive than the name 'dictionary' tends to imply. As such, they can be almost indistinguishable from encyclopaedias and we will deal with both together. Rebecca's favourite dictionary is the *New Fontana Dictionary of Modern Thought* edited by Allan Bullock and Stephen Trombley. Debbie and Jane's favourite is the quirky and individual *Keywords* by Raymond Williams.

Most often, well established scholars edit such books. You may be invited by them to contribute a short piece for such a work on a specific topic or topics. Whilst it might not be high-profile and prestigious research publication, there can be real advantages in saying 'yes'. First, it exposes you to the discipline of writing concisely, authoritatively, accurately and comprehensively. Second, it may give you the opportunity to work with people who are considerably more experienced and senior than you. This can help to provide you with valuable networking opportunities. Third, if you are a struggling doctoral student, you may be motivated by the prospect of the (usually small) fee that you will receive for the work and/or the prospect of getting a courtesy copy of what will probably be quite an expensive book. Fourth, a dictionary or encyclopaedia entry can be a welcome addition to the CV/résumé of an emerging academic.

Reference guides

We think that the introduction to *The Blackwell Companion to Social Theory* edited by Bryan S. Turner provides the best possible definition of this type of book:

> *The Blackwell Companion to Social Theory* intends to provide a comprehensive introduction for a general audience to major developments in social theory.

That is, reference books don't set out or develop new knowledge but rather seek to provide comprehensive explanations of existing understandings in a manner that is accessible to those not already familiar with a particular field of enquiry at an advanced level. They are the sort of books to which people turn when they are first 'getting into' a subject and need a general but sophisticated introduction.

They usually contain a number of specially commissioned chapters, each of which addresses an aspect of the field. Whilst these will often be written by well established researchers, the editor may view the volume as a development opportunity for some less senior academics and also invite them to contribute. Equally, a commissioned author may invite a less experienced colleague to join them in writing such a piece. If you get either of these types of invitation you should take it as a vote of confidence in you and an excellent opportunity. If you are the right person for the job then it should be bread-and-butter work, done only at marginal cost, and a synthesis of or exposition on what you already know.

Annotated bibliographies

There is an annotated list of suggested Further Reading at the end of each book in the *Academic's Support Kit* that you can use as an example of this genre. It is, however, rare to see whole books consisting of annotated bibliographies. The key to a good annotated bibliography is to ensure that it gives a succinct and accurate account of the books it describes, says something about their intended readership and comments briefly on how successful they are. Making a good selection of books to be annotated is also important, and this means that if you have been asked to do one, you need to ensure that your selection is fit for the purpose for which it was intended.

Books for Beginners

There are several series of books intended for people who want to learn something about a completely new subject in an entertaining way. One of the best known of these is the ... *for Beginners* series in which experts in different areas write pithy, witty introductory texts, usually illustrated with cartoons, about a whole series of issues and ideas. Titles in the series include topics as far apart as *Feminism for Beginners* and *Judaism for Beginners*. We like these books quite a lot and imagine that the authors make quite a lot of money, but we have never been asked to write one ourselves and it is unlikely that you will be either. Unless you find their style relatively easy to attain, you are probably better off steering clear of such books.

The digitisation of scholarship

There is much you need to know about the digitisation of scholarship, particularly around the politics and what they mean not just for you but also for the public's access to knowledge.

The changing nature of publishing

We are in the midst of a virtual revolution in scholarly publishing. More and more scholarly (i.e. peer-refereed) journals are now available on-line and as well as in hard copy. Some are available on-line only, some are open-access and some you have to pay for in one way or another. At the same time, many of the big print publishing houses are getting together stables of scholarly journals. Furthermore many publishing houses have 'added value' to such journals by providing a range of additional services. These include such things as email alerts to the table of contents of new issues, hyperlinking, author and topic searches of data bases, hits and download data provision and archives of material about particular topics.

What does this mean for scholarly practices?

These changes have, inevitably, led to a shift in the practices of scholarship. Academics actually go to libraries less and less, because we can access so many journals on-line – both those that our libraries sub-scribe to and those that are open-access. Indeed, some literature suggests that if articles are not on-line, readers are becoming less inclined to chase them up in hard copy. As the editors of *Nature Magazine* (397, 195–199. http://www.uibk.ac.at/sci-org/voeb/nat.html) say:

> The ability to click from an abstract or citation to the full text of an article is prompting a shift in the way that journals are used. Scientists often care less about the journal title than the ability to track down quickly the full text of articles relevant to their interests. Increasingly, users view titles as merely part of hyperlinked 'content databases' made up of constellations of journal titles. As a result, the competitive edge of publishers is increasingly coming to depend on their ability to muster a critical mass of attractive information through a single powerful and user-friendly interface.

There are many benefits for academics and for journals if they publish within the publishing stables of the big publishing houses, not the least being the enhanced international visibility, citability, intellectual presence and potential impact that such a home brings with it. This is an especially important issue for researchers outside the USA, Europe and UK who have to struggle for recognition by UK, European and US publishers and scholars. The more journals that join these publish-ing houses, the more they can add value and the more academics are likely to access their particular 'databases' as their major knowledge sources. This leaves other journals and indeed other publications in a vulnerable position. Unless they have a strong presence in other international abstracting and indexing systems they run the risk of becoming invisible and residualised in the globalising research scenario.

So what are the issues and concerns?

There are a number of far-reaching implications to think about in relation to the digitisation of publishing, which revolve around matters of access to and control of knowledge.

- All publishing houses are taking digital publishing and scholarship very seriously. Those particularly involved in it include Reed Elsevier, the Canadian Thomson corporation Wolters Kluwer, Wiley, Springer and Blackwell. Such companies are putting together huge electronic archives of intellectual property and are in competitive tension with each other (and sometimes swallowing each other) seeking to own all books, archives and research journals. ('Knowledge Indignation: Road Rage on the Information Superhighway', http://www.abc.net. au/rn/talks/bbing/stories/s345514.htm, accessed 12/8/2001). Why? The answer is the potential for profit.
- At this stage university researchers may be able to access various databases free of charge, but our university libraries, with their dwindling budgets, are being charged considerable amounts – not just for individual journals but also for bundles of journals, only part of which may be wanted.
- Of course, the more journals the publishing house has, the more it will be able to charge. And once it has a monopoly in a particular field the opportunities for additional charges increase. Perhaps we will soon see charges by the page or by viewing time. The potential is there for viewing, sharing and downloading opportunities to be further restricted and to be increasingly costly.
- If you don't have access via a library you may not even be able to access abstracts, and each journal article costs a considerable amount.

In essence, then, we are seeing the increasing commodification and privatisation of public knowledge in the digitising and globalising intellectual bazaar. While distribution may be enhanced, access may become more and more restricted as it becomes more and more costly. This is a particularly important issue for poor nations. And, equally, the control of knowledge slips yet further from the hands of those who produce it and from those who fund those who produce it, namely the taxpayers.

In terms of the issue of public knowledge the following irony arises. Knowledge is produced by public money in the form of research and of journal editing and other refereeing services but then locked away in the profits of private publishing houses. The research published in the journals is most often funded by government money but certain profits go to international or global companies. Governments thus pay thrice: they pay to produce the knowledge, to 'quality assure' it and then to buy it back. Even notions of the knowledge economy are caught on the horns of competing needs:

- One, to expand the public knowledge base as much as possible.
- And, two, to commercialise that knowledge.
- Three, to keep the benefits of that knowledge in the national interest.
- And, four, to globalise it.

Responses in the academic and policy community

Many research projects, journals and websites and various stakeholders and interest groups are examining the issues associated with on-line scholarly publishing. Groups include international information technology companies, economists, librarians, lawyers and vice-chancellors, the Association of Research Libraries and the Scholarly Publishing and Academic Resources Coalition (SPARC). Some examples follow.

- The Public Knowledge Project at the University of British Columbia is exploring all these issues, and all who publish should regularly visit their site, which is to be found at http://www.pkp.ubc.ca/.
- The dangers of the commercial scenario in the market for science, technical and medical journals led scientists to be so concerned they established a lobbying group called the Public Library of Science (see 'Background Briefing', Radio National, 12 August 2001) They also publish open-access journals such as *Pubmed*, the *Journal of Insect Sciences, eScholarship* and *Documenta Mathematica*.
- Various professional associations, societies and other groups and individuals continue to publish open-access, peer-refereed and quality-controlled knowledge on line. They are getting into the pertinent international indices such as Ingenta and are also seeking to provide all the value-added features that are now available through the big

publishing houses. In education, for example, Gene Glass, from the USA, operates the highly popular and respected open-access and peer-reviewed *Education Review* and *Education Policy Analysis Archive.*

The matters debated in these forums include:

- New alliances for the delivery of scholarly information.
- The role of libraries and librarians.
- Electronic access versus ownership of information.
- Subscriptions and new pricing models.
- Information intermediaries.
- Society versus commercial publishing.
- Mergers and acquisitions in the publishing industry.
- Authorship.
- Readership.
- Archival access to electronic information.
- Digitising the past.
- Peer review.
- Self-publishing.
- Copyright.
- Open access.
- Escalating costs and consequent cuts to libraries holdings.
- Particular difficulties for poor to middle income countries (although some big publishers now give developing countries open access to top medical journals).
- How academics can control their own publishing processes, to ensure top-quality low-cost publishing.
- What alliances might best facilitate this?

(Thanks to the person who developed this list. We are still trying to locate their name and the source.)

Professional and wider dissemination (non-academic writing)

Finally, we want to talk about the dissemination of your work to professional and wider audiences through non-academic writing.

Whether this is for you or not is, in part, dependent on your discipline. If you work in a vocational field, such as health-related subjects or education, then writing for professionals will be a necessary part of your work.

These fields of enquiry all have their own professional journals, which may be more or less well respected within the profession. In some cases there is crossover between professional and research journals. For example, both doctors and medical researchers read journals like the *British Medical Journal* and *The Lancet*. In other fields the professional journals are separate from the academic ones but they are still worth writing in for two reasons. First, it is a way of disseminating your work more widely in order to make an impact on practice. Second, it can be used to provide evidence in your CV/résumé that your work is relevant and that you have the esteem of people who may use your research in their practice as well that of your academic colleagues.

Do not, however, fall into the trap of thinking that writing for professionals is a substitute for, or the same as, writing in academic refereed journals. If yours is a field that requires such writing, you need to remember that it is a very different generic form from the refereed journal article. In writing for a professional or lay audience you must pay careful attention to its needs and to the requirements of the publishers and editors of your work. It is important to be accessible and not to assume that lay readers will understand academic phraseology and jargon. If you have to use technical terms, explain them and give understandable examples of what you mean.

It is also worth writing about your research for serious newspapers from time to time. Before you do so, however, you need to speak to the relevant editor and agree on the word length and what you are going to write about. Newspapers have very strict word limits and will not publish articles that are longer than they have commissioned. Anything written for a newspaper needs to be very accessible, brief and to the point. Editors of newspapers will not worry about changing your article in order to make it shorter or more understandable, so if you want it to appear the way you wrote it you must adhere to an appropriate style and agreed length. It is also imperative to stick to the deadline you have been given.

There are three good things about writing for the serious press: first, it's a good discipline to have to explain yourself briefly and clearly; second, you will have a much wider audience than you could in any other way; and finally, you will be paid for your work.

And finally ...

As this book has demonstrated, the business of writing and publishing is complicated, demanding and problematic. In contradistinction, it is one of the things that provides academics with a real and enduring sense of achievement and satisfaction. One of us was recently having a difficult discussion with a manager. We mentioned that we had a new book out that day. The manager looked wistful and a little sad and said, 'Oh, that must be nice, to have a book published.' Remember that, for all the hard work and sweat, and all the pressures that we are under to do it, it is still one of the most rewarding things an academic can do. Don't let anyone take that sense of satisfaction away from you, ever.

Further Reading

Clark, R. and Ivanic, R. (1997) *The Politics of Writing*, London: Routledge. This book argues that writing is a social practice and is tied to relations of power. It looks at how some forms of writing are given more prestige than others, how writing is a struggle for all writers, no matter how experienced, and how writing and identity are interconnected. Writing is seen as a resource for thinking and learning. The book draws attention to the ways that a piece of writing is shaped and constrained by the anticipated audience. Clark and Ivanic argue that writing is far more than a mechanical skill and they draw on social theory, cultural studies, media studies, semiotics, discourse analysis, linguistics, literacy studies and composition studies to make connections between these different fields to deepen their understanding of writing. They examine writing as a political act, the social context of writing and use examples of 'real writing' to illuminate the points they make.

Golden-Biddle, K. and Locke, K.D. (1997) *Composing Qualitative Research*, Thousand Oaks CA, London and New Delhi: Sage. The authors are concerned that the practice of writing is not addressed, in terms of supporting doctoral students but also in relation to professional academic writing. The aim of this book is to 'demystify writing to enhance our own and our intellectual communities' abilities to contribute knowledge'. Their audience is those studying or working in the field of organisational and management studies. The book draws on the metaphor of 'story' to explore the issues involved in writing for management journals. They explain: 'the issue in writing up qualitative research, then, becomes not whether we tell stories but rather how conscious we are of the stories we tell.' This requires writers to examine their theoretical positions and the way they develop it in their writing. Writers need to explore both what they write and how they write. The authors challenge the notion that writing reflects objective reality. Rather both the writer and the reader shape the text.

Ivanic, R. (1998) *Writing and Identity: The Discoursal Construction of Identity in Academic Writing*, Amsterdam and Philadelphia: Benjamins. This is an important book that explores the relationship between identity and academic writing. It starts from the position that the writer is not a neutral objective individual writing up the objective results of research. Rather the writer is socially located and brings their identity positions, experiences, values and interests to the writing. Ivanic's overall argument is that 'writing is an act of identity in which people align themselves with socio-culturally shaped possibilities of selfhood, playing their part in reproducing or challenging dominant practices and discourses, and the values, beliefs and interests which they embody.' Although the book theorises writing, rather than it being a handbook for writers, it is useful for those wanting to explore the relationship between themselves and the writing that they produce. Part II is less theoretical, as it draws on the writing that different people have produced to illustrate the theory in Part I. It argues that understanding writing as intimately connected with self and identity can help us to write. One way into the book, suggested by Ivanic herself, is to begin with Chapter 6, which presents a case study and brings the issue of writing and identity to life.

Richardson, L. (2003) 'Writing: a method of inquiry' in N. Denzin and Y.S. Lincoln (eds) *Collecting and Interpreting Qualitative Materials*, Thousand Oaks CA, London and New Delhi: Sage. This is a valuable contribution to thinking about the central role of writing in qualitative research as a methodology in itself. The chapter challenges the conventional approaches to writing qualitative research because, unlike quantitative research, which can be presented in tables and summaries, qualitative research 'carries its meaning in its entire text' and has to be read. Richardson points out that although she writes to learn she was taught 'not to write until I knew what I wanted to say, until my points were organised and outlined'. This is a problem, as are conventional approaches to writing tied to 'mechanistic scientism' because it overlooks the creativity of writing, it undermines new writers of research and it does not produce interesting texts. Richardson examines the historical contexts of writing conventions and then explores the possibilities of new modes of writing qualitative research, including 'creative analytic products'.

Woods, P. (1999) *Successful Writing for Qualitative Researchers*, London and New York: Routledge. This book focuses on the writing of qualitative research, in relation particularly to symbolic interactionism and education. It argues that although we have reached a new, postmodern moment in qualitative research, traditional approaches to writing remain hegemonic in both the thesis and published academic articles. However, Woods argues that 'the scope for experimentation is gradually widening' and for a creative approach to academic writing leading to new modes. The book explores the following issues: the psychology of writing and the 'pains and perils of writing', common modes of organising the writing of qualitative research (i.e. by category and/or theme), new modes of writing, the process of editing, new technologies in writing and writing for publication.

Index